A HEALTH CHECK FOR YOUR BUSINESS

A
HEALTH
CHECK
FOR YOUR
BUSINESS

JOHN F GITTUS

KOGAN
PAGE

First published in 1993

Kogan Page Limited
120 Pentonville Road
London N1 9JN

British Library Cataloguing in Publication Data

A CIP record for this book is available from the British Library.

ISBN 0-7494-0875-8

Typeset by Saxon Graphics Ltd, Derby
Printed and bound in Great Britain by Clays Ltd, St Ives plc

Contents

Introduction

Every day we hear of businesses going to the wall, individuals becoming bankrupt and of unwelcome company take-overs.

Those that continue unscathed must be spurred on from time to time by this chilling news, determined to avoid a similar fate.

What comfort can they take as they glance over their shoulders at the trail of devastation left behind? By what criteria do they judge their own positions? Just how safe are they today, and indeed, what does the future hold for them?

This book is not about crystal-ball gazing into the future as influenced by the stars or other external phenomena. It uses well tried and tested business analysis techniques and will enable the reader to look deeply into the well-being of his business as it stands today, and as it faces the future.

It will assist in exposing any weaknesses which require attention and comfort you in identifying the strengths that you have built. Its thoroughness will surprise you, and by the time you have completed it you will be both inspired and comforted in the knowledge that your operation has been through the most methodical and searching health check to which it could be subjected.

Those with high responsibilities in business, owners and students alike will benefit from reading this work. So too will expansionist companies wishing to measure the intrinsic worth of target operations before bidding. Those responsible for funding industry, such as bankers, will find that the contents will guide them in assessing their risks in a detail far beyond that available from a mere collation of statistical information. The book presents them with a vast area of subject matter to be explored with their clients.

Financial analysts will find the work useful in looking behind the figures, past trends and six-monthly statements into the matters that really make a company tick and determine its future.

First and foremost the book is written for the business manager with line responsibility for part or the whole business or commercial operation.

The safest way to succeed in business and avoid unwelcome take-over bids is of course to be highly efficient in all areas. This book will help those responsible in all sectors of business, whether public or private, to achieve those high standards of excellence.

Above all it should give the reader the assurance that he has measured his efforts and his progress against the most exhaustive business health review possible; that he is aware of the status and direction of his operation from every important aspect.

1

Self-Appraisal

Personal values

What motivates me?

It is often assumed that people enter business with one simple objective in mind – to make money!

But we know that many could earn far more if they gave up their own efforts and merely became employed elsewhere. For these people independence is a vital factor. Far better, they argue, to be their own boss than to take orders from another even if their financial reward is less. For these people, of which there are thousands, to be 'their own boss' is the most compelling of all motivations even though they may be a one-man band.

Perhaps a main inspiration is to make enough money so that an early retirement may be possible. Hard work now for more leisure time later in life? The game plan here may be to build a successful business during a short career with a view to selling it for a retirement nest egg at the appropriate time.

For some this may have been the original intention but the adrenaline of business management may have taken over so much that it is all pervasive. If other interests have been blocked out over the years you may not be able to face the vacuum that may arise if you quit, or it may even become a virility test.

One high-powered executive known to the author was once voicing his intentions to stay in business until the end. He felt that his father had retired too early (in his eighties!). Reflecting on this he claimed his father would probably have reached a century had he not chosen 'premature' retirement.

This individual is following closely in his father's footsteps and still going strong. His financial incentive to work must have been satisfied many years ago although it is always useful to have more!

The individual may be motivated by excellent financial incentives of a public nature such as grants, cheap finance, or low-rental properties in enterprise zones or development areas.

The job location or any one of a number of external factors may inspire them.

Some personal impediment may make it difficult for a particular person to gain employment elsewhere. Family responsibilities may take preference or the distance of travel from the home.

Many that go into business are driven by the respect given them by others. It may be a matter of self-respect or the admiration of family and friends. It could serve another purpose altogether, such as the kudos derived from business activities when running for public service.

Some keep trading in order to keep themselves young or active. This is often the case when bringing up a family late in life. The need to go off to the office each day, like younger parents, watched by the children, can be persuasive.

Many thrive on the power that their position gives them over others, be they employees, their peers or the world at large. This is a much stronger motivation than one might imagine. Many enjoy it without necessarily abusing it, but then again this leads to value judgements and moral interpretations. What one person sees as abuse is not seen in the same light by another.

For some the incentive is to keep alive the tradition of their family business, or create one for the next generation. Many such businesses are worth millions. Take, for example, sheep farmers in Wales owning huge stocks and vast acreages of land. In theory many of them could sell up and live on the proceeds for the rest of their lives, but they are not likely to because of the expectation that their children will inherit this business in the same way that they and many generations did before them.

To many business people there is something deeply satisfying derived from giving employment to others, but they do not always receive due recognition when it is necessary to lay off workers.

The product or service of the concern in itself may be reward enough. There are many products in industry that give the producer and those connected a sense of philanthropic values. Better to be producing a health product, such as spectacles giving sight to many, than items of mass destruction.

The element of danger is the main driving force for some. Perhaps it is the excitement of meeting famous or important people, or being hooked on the inherent interest in the product. For a lucky minority their hobby becomes their business, or at least a spin-off. This might apply to tennis players, artists, professional chess players and so on. They may sell or endorse the utensils or output of their sport or other interest, produce the lead magazine for their hobby and derive enormous additional reward from their involvement.

We hear much of 'workaholics'. What drives them if it is not the financial reward? It may be they have such a tidy mind that they cannot bear to be behind with their work. It may be work is a substitute for other interests in life for which they feel a void. They could simply just love work for its own sake. Why not?

There can be many benefits to owning your own business beside the dividend or salary that you receive. You may enjoy the entertainment side, meeting people, taxation efficient remuneration packages, fixing your own hours and conditions of work and so on.

There are many more general reasons that motivate people into management and business in their own right. They are not mutually exclusive and often come together more by accident than design. As circumstances change these too may change.

The more time spent in business the less will be available for other pursuits. This leads us to consider the total values that we have in our lives as a whole and the opportunity cost of the other activities that we might wish to select.

What must be clear is that the matter is most complex and it does not lend itself to a quick answer.

The health of your business can only be measured in the very widest sense if its performance satisifies the criteria by which you yourself judge success. You could ask 'Healthy for what?'

Before reading on reflect on this and see how far you are able to recognize your own motivations and personal values from the foregoing. This will help you to put the rest of this book in context. You will be able to take a more balanced view of the operation for which you are responsible when it comes to measuring its success and its state of health.

You may not have subjected yourself to this kind of assessment before. Doing so now may well influence the direction you take in responding to the identified needs of the operation.

What is my investment risk?

People do not find themselves drawn into business without taking some risk. Let us attempt to establish what you have at risk in your business. If this is very material then you will be all the more concerned to ensure that it is in good shape.

The non-financial risks may involve your personal health, the possible stigma and stress attached to failure and the regard had for you by your family or peers. In fact these risks may be associated with the loss or diminution of any of the motivations we have discussed above.

What about the financial commitment? If bank finance is involved there is a good chance you will have given security on your own home or other appropriate assets. In this case the failure of the business could mean you find yourself homeless or even bankrupt. The only way to avoid this pressure may be to build up a successful venture, by whatever it takes, in order that you may sell it as such on the open market.

You will probably have subscribed part or all of its share capital, and will know how much this cost you. There may also be personal assets in use in the business.

Consider whether you have waived any fair salary or other benefits by way of an indirect investment, and be honest with yourself when summarizing your full financial involvement.

Ask yourself again what you stand to lose if there were no business. This is unlikely to be the same as your original investment. Apart from the securities given and monies subscribed, the open market value of the business will presumably have increased in its own right. To answer this question, in effect, is to attempt to value the business on the open market. You might require some specialist advice as to its worth (see *What Is Your Business Worth?* Geoffrey Dalton, Kogan Page, 1992), the acid test always being what a potential purchaser would be prepared to pay.

If you own a part of the enterprise and not the whole then the principles apply in much the same way for that fraction.

Your financial commitment does not have to be associated with an investment already made. It could be the future reward that you anticipate in due course from your labours. It will pay you to distinguish between monies already sunk or committed to the business and those to do with future expectations.

By now you should have a fairly clear idea of what motivates you, and what you have at risk. These are the main bench marks which will influence your future actions. You may wish to write them down below to serve as a catalyst for future action:

	Non-financial	*Financial* £
Motivations		
☐		
☐		
☐		
Investment risks		
Already pledged	—	
Current business value	—	
Future expectations	—	_____

Human capital value

In completing the above table, in the first instance, you will probably have considered the business as you know it today. It is when you contemplate future benefits that you recognize its dynamic character, and realize that it may be quite changed in time to come. Most hope that this will indeed be the case because this is their main driving ambition.

At this stage you may only have answered this in terms of your own aspirations, and this is all you should concentrate on at present.

The business will of course be capable of going in various directions with entirely different results in terms of ultimate value. You are no doubt in the driving seat, but the intrinsic value and future potential owe much to the management as a whole, technicians, employees with historical and specialist knowledge and all those who work with and for the operation. The sum of all this is known as its *human capital value*, and this, as much as anything else, will determine its future value.

It is true that this is constantly changing and being moulded anew by the introduction of new blood, and sometimes through the loss of key personnel. The effective use of this most important of all assets is crucial to the future. Much will depend upon the loyalty of personnel and this is only ignored at your peril.

Think of the business as an entity apart from yourself. If you were to leave or sell it to an outsider then it is the 'human capital' engine-room that will determine where it goes without you.

There is no scientific way of valuing human capital except in that any value attributed to the business now, or in the future, cannot exist without it.

The performance of people within the enterprise therefore determines its health as much as any other factor. At the centre of this is the style and quality of management with which most of the remainder of Chapter 1 is concerned.

Return on capital employed (ROCE)

Of all the motivations considered by individual readers it is unlikely that many will have disregarded the basic aim of financial reward. This, after all, is what a free enterprise society is all about.

The traditional way of measuring success with any investment is to calculate the return on capital employed. This concept is central to the issue and requires some explanation. We all know what is meant by the return on our money if we simply make a deposit with the Post Office or a building society. It is measured by the rate of interest received, the greater the better! There will be an extra payment if the deposit is committed for a longer term, or if it is more worthwhile in terms of its size.

There is usually no risk involved with such transactions, but if the investor thought there was then he would decide against that institution in favour of another, unless of course a slightly higher reward was available to persuade him to make the investment!

This may, for example, be offered by a new entrant in the investment market (or a less well established concern) in order to generate business. There is clearly some greater element of risk involved, and this introduces the most important concept – that the rate of return can only be judged commensurate with the risk involved.

Investments can of course become both more risky and more complicated. At the next level you may invest in bonds and gilt-edged securities. At the next level again you may be a shareholder in a company in which you have no management role. This may be in a more or less risky sector of industry, not to mention the ups and downs of the economic cycle and individual company success.

You would certainly be looking for a better level of return than that earned comparatively safely from the building society. It will not come exclusively from dividends, but also from an increased share price which will reflect the company's general performance, future expectations, its supporting assets and the reserves retained in the business.

No prudent business pays out all it earns in dividends. This is just one reason why the return measured in the hands of the shareholder is not an appropriate yardstick to apply to the financial efficiency of the trading operation.

To apply the concept of return on capital employed to a trading operation, consider initially the building society investor. Then substitute his lump sum deposited for all the assets of the business, and the interest received for the profits of the business. In its simplest context the return of these profits on the assets used (also expressed as a percentage) is the return on capital employed. It is the most appropriate measure of the financial success of a trading operation.

There are important differences between the return on capital employed and the other concepts so far discussed:

- First, ROCE does not relate the profit return to the proprietor's initial investment in the business. It is concerned with the total assets employed however and by whoever these are financed today.
- For practical purposes profits are averaged over the period of measurement to iron out fluctuations – usually expressed over one year.

- ROCE has no regard to the level of dividend paid out because this is not a correct measure of the overall profitability, influenced by it as it may be.
- The capital employed comprises the fixed assets and the net working capital of the company at balance sheet values. These sometimes include property revaluations and other such adjustments to ensure that the return can be more accurately compared with the alternative investments. The net working capital will be the sum of the trade assets less trade liabilities.
- In this context bank overdrafts do not form part of the trade liabilities because they are merely one form of finance used to support the investment in the same way as shareholders' capital, external loans and other sources.
- Profits used in the equation are stated before charging interest on any form of funds because this would invalidate the very calculation itself. It may be a matter of preference or historical accident whether the capital employed is wholly financed by shareholders' funds, borrowed monies or a compromise. We are looking here for a measure of financial efficiency of an operation that can be universally applied without regard to this variety of funding method. It is the return that it generates that is being measured, and not the choice or accident of its distribution.
- The profits will be stated over the year after charging depreciation on assets. For shorter periods they will be 'annualized' in order to find the yearly rate of return.
- Finally, the profits are normally stated gross before taxation for comparison with other investments, but the relative rate of tax will be a consideration.

In Chapter 2 we set out a typical balance sheet and summary profit and loss statement under the title 'The total business thermometer', which will be used to illustrate the calculation of the all-important return on capital employed and other key pointers to the financial health of a business. It will also be used to illustrate the main methods available to improve profitability.

Summary
- We have considered what motivates us personally in business, and the risks already taken.

- The essential human capital value has been recognized for further discussion.
- We have recognized at an early stage one of the most important universal means of measuring the financial health (the return on total capital employed) that we will be using to evaluate our current and future performance.
- We have now identified the crucial financial motive that acts as the common denominator for all the others at the centre of all business activity.

Management methods

Management types

The health of any business depends on the skills of its management team, yet the style and approach of one manager may be quite different from those of another.

Which types get the best results? Which type are you and the other members of your particular management team?

First there is the severe and formal manager, the kind that causes staff to quake at his very footsteps. He will bark out his orders, usually spending little time to assist or explain. A few quick dismissals before lunch will set him up for the rest of the day. He will never take other members or employees into his confidence and he sees enemies around every corner. In short, he is a commercial bully.

His bark may be worse than his bite and his personality may have some saving graces. However, his employees may have enormous confidence in him. They feel secure that there is somebody who knows what he wants and saves them the strain of responsibility. His eccentricities may be no more than expected and he may even be loved for them.

In contrast there is the type that leads by example. No task will be given to anybody unless he can first understand it himself. He will take time to explain the rationale for his decisions, will be a good instructor and not beyond rolling up his sleeves to tackle menial or undesirable tasks. He will not bark out his instructions and his enthusiasm could carry troops over the top into battle.

Of course, he may not be respected for all this. It is often the case that he will be taken advantage of by his staff and by external contacts. A 'mister nice guy' image does not always get its just reward.

The author recalls an occasion when a candidate for the board was slated for personality defects prior to his appointment. Believing that nice guys do not survive at the top, the chairman commented, 'He should fit in very well then', upon which his appointment was duly accepted.

Some management types stubbornly refuse to delegate. They keep their cards very close to their chest since to delegate may be to teach their juniors the secrets of their job, and weaken their own positions. They are more likely to end up being workaholics and they do not serve their businesses well. If they are ill, or leave, then there is no in-depth management skill left behind. This can lead to severe damage.

Those good at delegation find they are best able to use their own management skills in the more critical areas, and they create an enthusiastic team in which all are working nearer to their optimum capacity. This not only creates job satisfaction and general efficiency, but also gives juniors the appetite to work hard for their own promotion.

Some are methodical and cover all eventualities, and others are totally disorganized. Some can exercise judgement. They are good at weighing up future probabilities and the best route forward. Others do not even want to look beyond next week.

There are many in business who are simply driven by the power of their positions. They are autocratic and ingenious at devising management structures and other methods through which they can impose their own will, regardless of the general consensus. They will divide and rule, setting one against another. As long as they and they alone make all the decisions, they feel content. They tend to take the acclaim for the good decisions, but hastily look around for a scapegoat for their mistakes.

Strangely enough, their power is often best preserved by the use of more committees, not less. Two-tier boards can be a good example of where the top board is filled with hand-picked non-executive colleagues. The autocrat will use this to keep his executive colleagues in check, while the top board will only be told what he wishes them to hear.

We hear a lot about the benefits of introducing non-executive directors to top boards these days. It can become a kind of closed shop, with those elected introducing their friends throughout the industry on a reciprocal basis. Some end up with more director-ships than they can competently handle.

When their skills complement each other it can bring much benefit to the companies they serve. If, on the other hand, they spread themselves thinly among scores of companies at the expense of executive members, you can expect trouble. At best this demotivates the executives, and at the worst it can shelter the autocratic practices we have discussed.

An ambiguous or unclear management succession plan is often a signal that somebody is protecting his position of power against all comers. The total absence of a plan is usually a sure sign. Such 'demi-gods' have no real desire for a self-defeating succession arrangement. Given the chance they will hold on to power long after they should have stepped down and handed over the reins.

They will often cite great victories, and rub into their hapless colleagues their position of power. They are unlikely to forgive anybody who threatens their strength or voices an opposite view, and yet they often profess to be seeking those capable of leading change. Heads frequently roll in the interests of retaining the status quo. For those seeking to earn their respect for differently held views it is like indulging in a game of Russian roulette. This will only succeed if they have sound arguments which are difficult to refute, good skills of persuasion and show no signs of fear.

Another sure sign is a trail of management that have given up and left of their own volition. When the man at the top eventually goes the whole management structure will be found wanting.

This attitude does not always manifest itself at the top. There are many power-thirsty examples lower down, and still plenty of evidence of 'empire builders' around. They will hold on to as many staff and functions as they can whether this makes sense or not, and they will eye those of their peers with greed and ambition – little to do with the best interests of the operation. They are not slow with suggestions which widen their sphere of operation at the expense of their colleagues. They chase titles as though they are going out of fashion.

There will always be those whose heart is not really in the job. They are often immersed in side attractions, may encourage office gossip and act as a catalyst for trouble and conflict. But never let it be said that a healthy level of interests and pastimes outside the business is a sign of lacking commitment.

There are those who create an atmosphere in which one is made to feel guilty by leaving the office on time. Many wait until the 'boss' goes before they feel brave enough to scuttle off themselves. To leave your office on time is often a sign of effective planning, delegation and hard commitment to a task well done. You should be able to enjoy your leisure, to return the next day refreshed mentally and physically for what lies ahead. There will always be those occasions where circumstances or particular responsibilities dictate otherwise, but if these are commonplace then something is wrong. By the opposite token, there is nothing so unseemly as the queue which forms to stampede out of the office the very second normal time is ended.

Where management style fails to motivate others, some managers are very good at the productive use of incentive schemes. They can cover up defects elsewhere. Some managers listen to what the work-force tell them and learn an enormous amount from this fountain of experience. Others prefer to remain aloof. There will be those who can inspire and are co-operative, and those who are completely irrational and obtuse.

On one occasion the author took great pains to decentralize the accounting and reporting procedures for the subsidiaries in a group that had just gone public. Management accountants were appointed with the intention that they should make a contribution through their membership of the various management teams. They were all qualified and had suitable industrial experience to offer. After a month or two, regular management control information had been developed and a meeting was called to consider progress. A dejected new appointee reported that, despite his position, he had been denied access to the meeting on the grounds that 'other shop-floor personnel had longer service records'. How obtuse can people get, or was it self-protection?

Perhaps the new financial discipline was seen as a threat rather than a positive contribution, to the line executive.

Recognition of your own style, and that of your subordinates and colleagues may prompt you to do something about exposed weaknesses.

You spend half your life in the office and have a profound effect on the lives of others. There are times when you have to hire and fire, and when control and discipline are essential. The task is hard enough without also being the conscience of the world, but if you can be naturally cheerful and civil to those around you it does much for the quality of life.

How do we manage?

We have considered a variety of management styles and will have made up our minds about the virtues and problems associated with them. So how do *we* manage?

Is there a bias within our organization towards one type or another, and does this manifest itself generally throughout the concern or within certain individuals (ourselves included)? How will we know if any change is called for, given that quite opposite styles can lead to the same degree of success.

It is probably fair to surmise that a happy and enthusiastic work-force is likely to succeed better than one which is simmering and militant. Use this as your thermometer. Read the signs. Step in quickly where damage is being inflicted. Do not be afraid to be self-critical and remember that we all have different attributes. Build on the strong ones. Identify those areas now which will affect the health of your department or business in the long term.

Meetings

Meetings can be a forum for most useful debate and future guidance. They can be action-orientated, so that all members leave with a clear idea of immediate priorities and urgent tasks. They can be visionary and inspiring, the engine-room of the concern.

They can be an unnatural setting in which each member takes his turn at speech making. Firmly held views may be repeated *ad nauseam* at each successive meeting. Departmental differences are frequently voiced and blame attributed for shortcomings.

So important is the need for some members to excel that matters that could have been voiced or resolved earlier are often stored fo delivery at the next meeting. There is also a tendency for trivia to creep in which has nothing to do with the matters for which meetings are designed.

They can end up as nothing better than a social gathering where trivia are discussed. The author once looked on in astonishment when husband and wife major shareholders spent the first 15 minutes of a meeting discussing the colour of the tea-set, the business already being in a state of collapse. Husband and wife teams can come unstuck and fail to fuse with other outside managers. The same pair were once debating an issue when the husband, under some pressure, tried to defuse the argument by promising – 'I'll discuss it with you later, dear, outside the meeting'. 'I'm a director of this company, and we will discuss it at the meeting', she retorted, knowing that any support she had would be dissipated if discussed on her husband's terms.

Certain styles of management do not live in harmony with formal meetings at all. The autocratic type of manager is likely to argue that they are divisive, merely going round in circles while he alone has responsibility for the decision. The same manager may use this very fault to his own benefit and regard meetings as some form of entertainment before he draws his own conclusions and dictates. 'Conclusions' is the effective word. If the debate genuinely airs all the plausible alternatives and influences the outcome then meetings are likely to be valuable.

They will be so if they are led by a good chairman or chief executive. It will be his responsibility to summarize the collective view of the meeting. If it is finely balanced, or he wishes to take responsibility for overruling a strong consensus, then it is for him to say so. In time he will be judged by the consequences if he is not pulled up by his colleagues earlier.

Meetings should normally bring together representatives of all the main disciplines in the business such as production, marketing, development, finance, service and so on. Some chief executives fill meetings with members from their own discipline. One such company was once congratulating itself on its achievements as a completely marketing-orientated board. As such it was in no position to judge itself until things went seriously wrong, and then it was too late. There are many such cases, unfortunately. An example was given above of a manager having a particular aversion to the financial discipline and as a result leaving out the management accountant from any collective meetings. While the situation lasted, it destroyed the whole objective of achieving a responsible decentralization of subsidiary activities.

If a matter discussed at a meeting does not involve all the members, or is likely to be complex, detailed and protracted, a sound practice is the use of a sub-committee, made up of those nearest the subject. A sub-committee chairman should be appointed with specific responsibility to report back to the main committee with the findings by an agreed time. Failing that, progress reports are essential.

Too many non-executive members at the parent board level can be a mistake. It all depends who appoints them, and whether the executive members have sufficient representation.

It is the strongly held view of many that meetings hinder the conduct of the business. Better to have a quick chat with the person or persons involved in the particular area than waste the time of the whole executive by chewing it over collectively. This will get the action agreed and through much more quickly and with least effort. This is a very sensible method of operating provided that anything of real consequence affecting major policies is then reported to the other key members. This may be informally or at the next formal meeting, when it should be properly ratified and minuted.

When a complicated or serious issue requires airing it should be the duty of the prime instigator to circulate a paper containing the requisite information and recommendations in sufficient time for the other members to digest ahead of the meeting. Regular control information is discussed in Chapter 2.

Minutes form an essential part of meetings. Those present should already have taken a quick note of the action expected of them individually. Circulation of the minutes shortly after the meeting will then serve as a checklist from which all can work. It is essential they be agreed formally at the commencement of the next meeting. They may very often misrepresent the conclusions of the committee, depending sometimes upon who writes them, but when agreed by the majority they should be accepted and acted upon by all, including dissenting minorities. They can always ask for their dissenting views to be minuted if the matter is of sufficient importance, but any confusion or ambiguity left in the minutes at this stage will be an open invitation for subsequent sabotage and divisiveness by the non-believers.

It is the job of the chairman to be vigilant to spot this when it occurs (because it always does) and to hold the team on the agreed path. If meetings are the engine-room then their mode of conduct will have much effect on the health of the operation.

Summary
Meetings should:

- only be called where collective discussion is necessary; where major policies and decisions are under review; if they serve as a catalyst for agreed action
- be prepared in advance save for unforeseen emergencies
- be held at specified intervals for the purpose of reviewing general progress and performance
- be properly minuted and binding until otherwise agreed.

They should not be:

- unbalanced with regard to disciplines
- used as a battlefield for inter-departmental grievances
- taking people away from key action without benefit
- serving as a speech-making forum for the ambitious
- serving only to duplicate previous dialogues and favourite contentions
- the tool through which the autocratic manager represents his views as those of the full meeting
- biased towards too many non-executives.

It will be very much up to the chairman of the meeting to ensure that the meeting deals first and foremost with relevant matters and priorities. His skill in weeding out duplicated or misdirected effort will be vital, as will his ability to keep alive a spirit of common purpose and harmony.

If he is skilled in the art he will see the speech makers coming and forestall their attempts to take the stand by delivering a series of pertinent questions before they get going. If he is really skilful he will hit on the head the contentious questions and announce the meeting closed before any speeches get under way!

Danger signs It is all too often a danger sign when the chief executive or managing director is also the chairman. Look out for these further potential health threats:

- An autocratic boss that is all-dominating and shuns debate
- A passive board of management
- A boss who loads the board with his own discipline, or allies appointed from outside
- The absence of a strong-willed finance man
- Shallow depth of management.

Now ask yourself if your meetings are good productive forums. Is their constitution correct? Have you identified areas of health risk requiring change?

Reaction management considered

The discussion on the conduct of business thus far assumes that businesses all plan ahead and divert problems before they arrive. If this is not possible then the assumption is that the risks may be known and a degree, at least, of contingency planning may exist, if only in the mind.

Often this planned approach is entirely absent and even intentionally disregarded. Some managements thrive on perpetual fire fighting. They react to problems as they arise rather than pre-empt them. They approach opportunities in the same manner.

They justify the approach by insisting that nobody can be successful at crystal-ball gazing, and that any attempt to do so is wasting valuable time best spent in dealing with matters that do arise.

It is their firm belief that skills in reacting correctly to current situations will hold the organization in good stead for the future provided they satisfy one or two key benchmarks.

This exemplifies at best a goal-keeper mentality, and in the worst cases is completely lacking in the forward judgement that is so vital to the health of any organization.

The role of planning

People who are naturally methodical do not need to be persuaded of the advantages of forward planning. Mistakes are made, it is true, with a pre-occupation for planning and there are common errors even in its terminology.

All accountants and financial people are instilled with the need for planning as part of their basic training. An accountant colleague once chaired a meeting of chartered accountants at a seminar held to discuss the role and benefits of corporate planning. He was very articulate and well practised in mounting persuasive arguments. At the end of the seminar he told me he had added his weight to the non-believers, and they called a vote to establish consensus. Amazingly, the audience, which consisted mainly of members of that profession, voted against the role of corporate planning. This was some years ago and his views may have changed, but it serves to indicate that even within the profession most responsible for its creation there are those who doubt its value.

All plans serve to identify main aims and expectations. They provide a route map for action, allow those responsible to organize the requisite space, people and other resources with which they are to be carried out.

Above all, they are only a blueprint. They are a framework within which management can think and act. The very process of planning highlights those ideas that cannot work so they can be weeded out. The result should be tenable and capable of achievement. A company should never plan its resources and actions around a 'pie in the sky' target that has no chance of being accomplished.

Once a tenable plan has been prepared it forms the basis for immediate action. It serves as a lubricant without which everybody would be running around headless. The very next day the disbelievers will say it will be wrong, and that nobody can read the economy satisfactorily, let alone have advance knowledge of the unforeseen. They are entirely missing the point.

If you have a quantified framework within which to plan you can measure the effect of future variations as you meet them. You are better equipped to determine the relevant measures that may be taken in mitigation. You will know how these stand to affect your liquidity planning and other resources, and if your planning is of a high quality you may have some ready-made contingency ideas to put in place.

Good planning disciplines come naturally to those who are methodical. Time after time success in business comes more surely to those who have that quality.

> *Summary*
> It is the experience of planning and dealing with divergences that teaches you much more about the business itself. It is an indispensable tool.

The compromise

There is of course a compromise between the planners and pure reaction managers, as neither is sound for the health of the operation without the other.

Together you have the best tools and skills that you can acquire.

If you become obsessed with planning to the extent that you never actually manage, the result will be failure. If you manage by fire fighting in a vacuum you are little better off. However, the very act of planning in itself will avert a later need for some fire fighting. Not to plan is to take unacceptable risks. Therefore the compromise wins and both skills have their place.

Terminology

It may help to make things clearer if the problems of terminology are revealed. The most commonly used terms include:

Budget
Plan
Result
Variance
Forecast
Rolling forecast
Target
Corporate plan
Strategic plan
Contingency planning
Flexible planning

An enterprise usually prepares its budget for 12 months broken down by period. Its balance sheet will reflect its assumed starting position, incorporate sales expectations, capital expenditure intentions, supporting manning, and purchased materials or goods and overheads which it will incur. It will show the result in revenue terms, liquidity (funding), and its closing balance sheet. There will be detailed supporting information of the levels of income and expenditure by item for each department head. This will be in sufficient detail so that variations can be easily identified.

This *budget* is its own *plan*. If it is not reasonably attainable then it may not be worth the paper it is written on. It will have taken some time to prepare and there is usually little value in preparing it more often than once annually.

It is true that there are some companies that make it a virtue to be so closely in line with plan that they rewrite their plan quarterly or even monthly so that by the end of the year they are shown to be exactly on course for the latest edition. What a waste of time.

Businesses with good housekeeping prepare statistical information on a regular basis for control purposes by the month, week, day or even more frequently if relevant. For example, they may monitor scrap levels in a process at very frequent intervals to avoid throwing more money away once a deviation is noted. They will produce monthly financial accounts containing a variety of cost information in the form of the actual (as opposed to planned) *results*. This information is usually set out alongside figures contained in the *plan* so that lessons can be learned from the *variances* and action taken.

While the *plan* or *budget* will not change during the course of the year we have already noted that changes in actual trading performance may have rendered it invalid in so far as it no longer represents any true expectation of the likely outcome for the year. The concern may be doing better or worse than its plan. The management may be taking steps to pull performance up to budget or measuring the consequences on liquidity and other areas of a budget over-performance.

As the year progresses there is a need to know what the year-end result is likely to be. This is accomplished usually by a monthly *forecast* prepared to take into account known changes already reflected in the results, those known to be in hand and those anticipated in the remainder of the year. Changes of a topical nature will first be reflected in the revised forecast each month. These are likely to be the main focus of attention, and some management accounts include a 'forecast change' column especially to ensure they are highlighted. They will focus attention on changes that have already taken place with the combined effect of those still anticipated, in so far as they affect the trading year. The *forecast* therefore becomes the most dynamic tool of the concern once the plan has been set and the trading year is under way.

The term *rolling forecast* simply means all the available information is used to collate the likely outcome of the next 12 months, ie not merely to the end of the current plan. As the year draws to its close it is useful to have a view that goes somewhat further forward, and it will form a useful starting point for next year's budget or plan once adjustments resulting from policy changes have been incorporated.

A *target* is not a budget, plan or forecast or any of the other things. It is what it says it is. The company may prudently budget for a given level of sales, but it may allow itself a margin of safety by giving sales respresentatives *targets* that they wish to be achieved and which in aggregate exceed this total level. They may base pay incentives on this level and give it more impact by insisting that the more conservative levels of the plan are not revealed to those working to the target levels.

A *corporate plan* will cover a period of more than just one forward trading year. It will usually be from three to five years. Its purpose is to look and plan for the longer term. It will be invaluable in planning and arranging funding requirements. It will contain all the information relating to the operation known from the base year, and forward expectations as influenced by views on the trade and economy and the *strategic aims* and *policies* of the management.

Bankers prefer to use the term *business plan* when they are calling for a business to show its forward intentions before agreeing to advance finance. Just like the budget (annual plan) it is a most useful framework within which parties can think, and around which discussions can be conducted. It is a pity that some will use this description when they really mean the shorter term annual plan, which can be confusing.

The expression *contingency planning* also opens up a fair area for confusion. Before the senior management adopts an annual plan or budget they will do well to produce alternative figures showing the result of a range of the most likely deviations. They will occupy some time stating how these will be dealt with in advance, and this may be more or less formal.

With the aid of computers and spreadsheets it is not too difficult to produce a range of outcomes so that a single budget can in fact be *flexed* to accommodate known likely variations – most commonly in the level of sales. This form of *flexible budgeting* makes the preparation of the single annual plan that much more valuable without detracting from its essential status.

The same techniques can be applied to the more forward looking *corporate plan*, but the further ahead you go the less value this holds. It is in this area particularly that the 'planners' fall victim to the sceptics and non-believers, and the reader will understand how this is possible given the number of terms and disciplines already discussed.

Indications of good staff management

Judgement
A methodical approach affects all areas of business, not least the probability of success in staff management.

The most important management skill is business acumen and judgement. Application is essential but it will be fruitless if it is not based on good, sound judgement. We now explore those other areas of application that will be indicative of the health of any operation.

Staff involvement
Staff are not robots, operated by being switched on and off. As human beings they need to be motivated, understood sympathetically, sometimes comforted and at times disciplined.

Speaking to staff and obtaining their ideas is an essential part of the planning process. It gives a two-way advantage: You learn and the staff are motivated.

This may be carried out by informal counselling, suggestion schemes or periodic formal meetings. A manager who keeps closely in touch with his staff, however junior, wins more respect than those 'faceless names that never appear'.

If your concern is neglecting this discipline it is likely that defensive practices are building up, together with hostile attitudes. Nothing spells more danger for your future health and progress.

Communication
The key to it all is good communication, and for sound reasons:

Staff motivation
If your staff learn about things that affect their welfare from third parties such as the press, competitors, travelling sales representatives or neighbours, they are likely to feel abused.

When it is possible to reveal matters of a confidential nature that will concern them, it is important that you do so. Some matters are confidential and must remain so for varying periods. Before the news is about to break, you should prepare a briefing note which you should double-check for its likely repercussions, presentation and content.

You should have an established method of informing your staff of developments and dealing with their response. Inform senior persons first unless all are informed simultaneously. This is often best accomplished at a meeting called specifically for the purpose. Take note of the response and make your views known with intelligent reasoned argument, or undertake to do so as soon as you are able. If matters have to remain confidential for commercial protection do not be afraid to say so and remain firm.

The staff will feel a much higher sense of involvement and motivation if you communicate the long-term aims of the company. There is no better means of generating a team spirit and a sense of purpose. It also goes a long way towards allaying fears that the firm may indeed have no future! If the staff believe that you are planning and communicating the company's future they are more likely to commit themselves to you in the same way.

Defensive situations

There may be circumstances when you are put on the defensive and have to respond. This can be in the conventional prepared way or sometimes it is opportunistic.

The author attended a board meeting some years ago when threats of going slow, refusing to work overtime or striking were in the air. As the meeting ended and the directors were disbanding a maintenance employee arrived and was going about his business repairing a radiator just at the exit to the boardroom, but his interest in what was going on was not entirely passive. The chairman, never slow to take an opportunity, waited until he was almost adjacent to the man. He gave the writer a knowing wink and then said in a firm but confiding voice: 'Remember, the moment there is any sign of non-co-operation suspend them all immediately without pay'.

There had not been any previous suggestion of this as might have been inferred from the remark, but the throw-away comment was entirely effective. The message was carried straight back to the shop floor (as he knew it would be) and nothing more was heard of the go slow threat.

Public statements

An established method of communicating financial results and other sensitive information to the Press, shareholders and public at large is essential. Anticipate the response and brief all personnel that they should not comment unless so appointed. The person or persons appointed to make the response should follow a line prepared in advance, and be drawn no further unless extremely experienced in rebutting provocative comments. Some media will always use these in an attempt to present an attributed story. It is therefore always wise to ensure the reporter acknowledges that the official response must not be attributed to any named person unless he is the head of the organization and seeking the publicity on sound grounds. If you are not careful you may be drawn into a personalized argument in the Press which is neither good for you or your company. It all depends upon the quality and integrity of the financial Press, most of whom behave responsibly.

It is always a problem to know just what financial and other confidential information should be given to employees. It may be contained in legislation but gives plenty of scope for interpretation. Companies often fear that one answer may provoke 10 more questions. It is often felt the information may be used against the firm for wage bargaining or such like. There are different pressures concerning financial institutions, shareholders and competitors. These are often in the opposite direction to employee pressures, and the more information that is given the more difficult it becomes to satisfy everybody.

Similar considerations apply at annual general meetings and other shareholder and institution meetings.

Different organizations will have different approaches and some will be much more open than others about communicating this information.

A compromise is to reveal as much as you need to satisfy the morale and interests of all parties as well as the relevant legislation, but without giving every last vestige of information. This is what happens in most cases, but you will need to be certain that you have thought it through and prepared well in advance.

Sloppy communication of vital information can lead to rumours, misinterpretation and other pressures that end up being extremely damaging and self-fulfilling. They can threaten the well-being and future of the operation itself.

Practical commercial considerations

If there is not good communication your organization cannot be efficient.

The wrong goods or labour may appear in the wrong place at the wrong time at enormous cost. To start with, therefore, work instructions and the requirements of daily routines must be well communicated. Systems have to be watertight and good conveyors of procedural requirements.

Communications with customers are all-important. How much business is lost because somebody receiving telephone calls fails to pass messages on clearly, clogs up the line or offends by their attitude? The telephonist is one of the most vital positions in the company and also the first line of enquiry by those that mean you no good. All messages must be conveyed by the quickest possible means. You may not want meetings interrupted by each phone call but if you are methodical you will have given clear instructions beforehand.

You must determine in each case that information reaches each recipient as quickly as possible and by the most cost-effective method. There will be those internally and externally who harbour resentment because they have been victims of poor communication. They are seldom slow in coming forward if you ask them.

If you want to know how healthy your communications are simply ask your staff, your suppliers and your customers. Better still, telephone yourself from outside!

Rates of pay and incentives

The best protection for the business will come from linking at least part of the remuneration package to performance. This could be company or individual performance. The more that can be involved this way the better, but be certain that you do treat the employees as human beings. It is true to say that some piece-work type incentive schemes can be very dehumanizing.

The same may apply to clocking on and clocking off. You judge whether these procedures are neccssary or whether their absence would lead to a better spirit and tangible gains.

There is little that concerns most people more than their rates of pay. More than the financial need comes the hurt if their skills and knowledge are undervalued.

It is usually far better to go for quality than quantity. If you pay the top rates for the job and responsibility you will be secure in the knowledge that your store of 'human capital' will stay in place and serve you well. They will outperform higher numbers of lower paid and constantly changing employees.

This advice is not given without regard to the financial consequences to the business. Better to lose a few heads to support the extra outlay than store up the troubles of an underpaid work-force. The extra motivation of those remaining will usually absorb the workload of any that are shed with room to spare.

Staff development and training

We have established that your staff are one of your greatest assets, if not the most important.

To get the best out of them requires that their skills and experience be developed. Once again, a methodical programme of training thought out in advance will serve better than one which is haphazard.

The traditional methods are:

- Apprenticeships and other courses
- On-the-job training by those more skilled
- Attendance at day release courses
- University sandwich courses
- Seminars
- Educational financial assistance
- Periodic review and discussion of progress.

The individual needs of each trainee should be specifically identified and matched with the requisite programme. Everybody can benefit from training from the most inexperienced junior to the chief executive. Do not be afraid to reveal that you too are undergoing training of one sort or another. It will earn respect as well as encourage.

If every employee is given tasks and responsibilities up to his or her level of capability it will speed their development into really productive individuals.

Do not pour money into training without the trainee contributing something towards the cost, however small. A personal financial commitment does much to concentrate the effort. A review of progress as the training proceeds is all-important. Awards and publication of success stories do no harm.

You may wish to provide for the cross-fertilization of training and work knowledge and ensure that each skill is covered by somebody else. Greater job satisfaction will result from trainees' involvement over a larger range of tasks.

Examine the existing training and development programmes in place. Look at one department at a time and consider over a set period each and every employee in the enterprise. A far healthier business will result.

Job descriptions
There should be no ambiguity where job responsibilities start and end. All but the most menial jobs should have a written

description and a copy provided to the employee. This should be reviewed when work progress is discussed, and updated to cover the inevitable developments and changes which will occur. An 'any other duties' clause is a useful precaution against the difficult and argumentative type.

If job descriptions are properly prepared they can serve to settle some arguments about 'who does what' and provide a defence against 'empire builders'. First and foremost they are part of the job contract and provide a basis upon which reviews can be conducted. Duties which have lapsed can be spotted by reference to this most useful document.

While a single self-employed contractor is not likely to indulge in this discipline, its absence in anything much larger is not a good sign of a healthy operation.

Attitudes

A healthy attitude will usually be reflected by a proportion of long serving employees. If your entire staff turn over every year or two this causes a break in continuity. Knowledge acquired by key workers cannot be stored in such a short time and passed on for the benefit of those replacing them.

Compile a chart to show the split of your employees by length of service:

Years	Number	%
Under 1		
1–2		
3–5		
6–10		
11–15		
16–20		
Over 20		
	————	————
		100
	————	

See how you compare with other local concerns and your industry. Comparable statistics will be available from a number of sources if you enquire. Past figures from your own operation should also be compared in order to detect a trend.

If more than 80 per cent of your work-force has been with you for less than two years you could have serious difficulties ahead if they have not already manifested themselves.

Compile an employment status chart along the following lines:

		Number of employees	
	Budget	*Current month*	*Previous month*
Production 1			
2			
3			
Development			
Buying			
Auxiliary departments			
Marketing			
Sales			
Accounts			
Secretarial			
Management			
Full time			
Part time			

	Number of employees	
Movements:	*Current month*	*Year to date*
Resigned		
Redundant		
Dismissed		
Retired		
Recruited		
Net movement		
Numbers absent		

Notes:
1. Part-time workers to be entered as full-time units 2. The departments should be shown according to your own organization arrangements

A bad attitude is not usually difficult to detect. Sullenness, poor punctuality, late attendance at meetings, refusal to respond to sudden peak requirements, militant displays and general disinterest and lack of cooperation are but a few.

A study of the above tables, once completed, will tell you a lot about the business.

Conduct a critical examination of your operation or your department and consider whether something needs to be done.

Your own quality of management will reveal itself in the attitudes of the staff. Quite the best means of inspiration stems from your personal attitude, and this is not usually well served if you adopt an arrogant and aggressive manner. If you have to bawl and shout to get results, sooner or later it will surely break down.

Succession

Succession plans are certainly a sign of good health. They must start at the top and work downwards or they have no meaning.

Firstly, do all that deal with the firm, internal and external, know who to approach in the absence of the boss? Has such a person been groomed responsibly to act in his absence?

There are those who will wish to expose a weak second-in-command, for devilment, out of jealously or whatever. They will invent a crisis in the absence of the boss for him to deal with, or approach him over a pet 'hobby horse' that the boss has rejected earlier. At worst they will play one against the other, misquoting them blatantly. Is this going on around you? It takes a good second-in-command to deal with these situations and to know when matters can wait and when he must take responsibility for a decision.

Decision-taking abilities are one of the key personal qualities in management. They include the ability to take decisions on an appropriate time scale and also the sense to know when not to take them.

If the concern has earmarked a second-in-command it will be no earthly use if no confidence is shown in him. There must be full communication – one of the other essential qualities discussed above.

Further down the line there should be clear succession plans for each key position. Sometimes there is a trial honeymoon period before a potential succession candidate is told that he is so regarded. During this time he will be showing his abilities in performing the tasks so far delegated to him.

This period should not be dragged on unduly, and the succession candidate must be told of the plans, not necessarily a commitment, for him at the earliest possible opportunity.

It is not wise to run more than one candidate in tandem for the same position. If you wish to maximize your position by doing so it has its own dangers, especially if the arrangement is merely used to engender competition without any real intention to promote. Such arrangements can be very divisive and are often motivated by the wrong objectives.

The ideal situation is one where people are already in place in a junior role where they are being deliberately groomed for succession. They will receive appropriate training and support and will be a party to the succession plans whether they are standing by to meet an emergency or working in expectation of full promotion to the senior role. Progress will be monitored at least once yearly and both sides voice their problems and reservations quite frankly. The candidate will first be invited to make his own observations about his progress and this leads to a healthier atmosphere than one in which he presents himself for criticism. This encouragement to candidates to plan and contribute to their own development will pay back handsomely.

Consider whether or not all key positions are covered by succession plans or not. Think what would happen tomorrow if any key manager were hit by the proverbial bus. Are you well organized in this respect from within or without?

Management work schedules

How well organized are you?

Work duties

Managers go about their responsibilities in different ways, some haphazard and others more organized. It should not be difficult to organize yourself so that no important matters are overlooked, and priorities are recognized and given the first demand on your time.

Checklists of all the things that you regularly do are a great help. So too is a wall calendar on which to mark up regular and periodic commitments in distinctive colours. If you also keep a checklist for the regular chores of your subordinates you are half way there.

In the course of day-to-day business, unforeseen matters will arise, some of which you will delegate to others. Keep a notebook with you in which you enter anything of consequence under the initials of each person concerned, and do the same for yourself.

These notes and checklists will serve to remind you which routine and non-routine tasks require attention, and by whom. Ensure that you speak to each of your immediate juniors every day and enquire at appropriate intervals as to progress being made. Add and delete entries in your work checklist as they are accomplished. This methodical approach will pay off. Remember that nobody can store effectively in their head the total position and that a haphazard approach to the daily routine will certainly result in missed priorities and omissions of potentially damaging proportions.

You may sometimes wish to call a meeting with all present in order to take an overall look at progress. This will review priorities and the work allocation. It will serve to create a team spirit and draw attention to those not pulling their weight. This peer pressure can be used to great effect, and is also used to bring those back in line that are trying to pull in the opposite direction to policies already established.

Systems

You should be well organized in all your systems. Ideally, they will all be committed to paper, best contained in a systems and procedures manual accessible by all.

Pre-printed forms are the very best conveyors of information and should contain within them instructions on their completion. Make them as simple as possible. This will circumvent the need for their users to enquire into the system each time. They are the simplest means of de-skilling jobs and raising productivity in the office and elsewhere.

Production planning

A well organized business will have sound procedures for scheduling and planning incoming supplies, and your own production if you are in manufacture.

You will know exactly the capacity you have in your plant (or plants) by product and individual specification. Moreover, you will have some idea of the capacity of your competitors and the industry as a whole.

You will know whether it is prudent to double-source your product or supplies, and whether you should have spare capacity under wraps for that emergency. Unused spare capacity can be a most expensive luxury and most organizations cannot be that ambitious. It all comes down to relative need and cost, but if you have never thought about it you are probably not sufficiently organized.

You certainly will not be planning overhead and selling resources which are out of line with your production capacity. This will at best be uncomfortable and at worst disastrous.

You should know at any time how many of each item you have in stock and their location. If you do not know this the rest of the organizing is of little value. A major firm which was one of the early users of computers used to book tyres out of production into a temporary location, and then book them into store once they arrived at the warehouse. Call-off records in the stores were used to prompt replenishment orders on the factory. Initially, this was in such a mess that the delays in the recording into the stores led the computer system to prompt orders that had only just been fulfilled. By the time the original batches were booked into stores the firm had a glut of the tyres it needed least and was starved of the ones it needed most.

It is one thing having a system on paper. You have to maintain it daily and know exactly what is going on if you are at all well organized.

How will you know if your scheduling and production planning procedures are effective?

- You will always meet deadlines
- You will not need to work overtime.

Consider the position in your business *vis-à-vis* these criteria.

Satisfying the customer
This goes much further than providing the customer with a high standard of product or service that works.

The customer will need to know from time to time what progress is being made, or may encounter some particular problem. What happens when he phones in to enquire? Can you find the relevant records and paperwork while he is on the telephone? A promise to phone back can leave him feeling desperate, but if you can give an immediate response you have his goodwill.

Who does what?

We have already argued that a good business should compile a list of all of the duties of each of its managers and senior staff.

It is of course necessary to ensure that each discipline in turn is covered by this allocation of duties without omission. A responsibilities checklist is a useful tool that may be used for this purpose. An example to complete and keep in the office is shown opposite.

Management qualities

Summary

What are the key management qualities, and do you have them in your business?

We have covered most of these in this chapter. A good manager will require the following attributes and personal qualities:

Motivation
Judgement and business acumen
Capacity to take decisions
Delegation skills
Negotiation skills
Leadership and communication skills
Training abilities
Methodical approach
Organizational skills
Planning abilities
Conscientiousness
Integrity
Personality and smart appearance.

Task	Manager	Reports to:	Review date:
Purchasing			
Plant maintenance			
Production scheduling			
Production control			
Quality control			
Estimating			
Costing			
Pricing			
Customer complaints			
Employee relations			
Recruitment and pay			
Marketing and advertising			
Sales			
Invoicing			
Management information			
Accounts			
Cash collection			
Treasury			
Security			
Future development			
Planning			
Properties and insurance			
Pension administration			
Taxation			
Company secretarial			
Meetings and minutes			
Other major roles			

Knowing precisely who does what is half way towards being well organized.

2

Appraising Your Business Today

Introduction

Chapter 1 studied the effect on the health of the business of those working within it, with particular emphasis on the management. It dealt with the store of human capital in personal terms and focused on those qualities that are indicative of a healthy and sound operation.

External organizations attempt to get some grasp of your standing in these areas, and indeed Chapter 1 may give them more clues where to look and where to enquire. Attention to these areas will have much to do with improving the well-being of the concern but they are not used in themselves, however, to measure results.

There are more obvious areas through which results can be assessed. First, there are the more tangible areas that can be discussed. You can talk about business efficiency in general terms, measure competitiveness, relative risks, offers of finance and others which are the result of your endeavours rather than the means through which they are carried out. Second, it is possible as an outsider to review the adequacy of your business controls. Opinion can be given regarding management control forms and reports in use.

Most importantly the outside world measures your success in terms of financial results and analysis prepared for your own use and for general publication. These statements represent the ground on which all your efforts are set out in summary form, audited by independent professionals.

It is upon these results that judgement will be passed, and will influence those who buy or sell your shares, or agree to finance the business or otherwise. This domain of financial results and analysis needs to be fully understood or all your efforts can so easily come to naught.

Business appraisal

The meaning of general business efficiency

General efficiency in business will lead to the ultimate financial measure of success: the profit return on capital employed. But what do we mean by general efficiency in business?

We in business, and those looking at our performance, will be familiar with a number of areas which are indicators of the level of efficiency.

For example, it is a sign of efficiency if we *always deliver our goods or services on time*. It will rebound on the financial success simply because a satisfied customer will place more orders. A high incidence of late deliveries will chase away sales altogether until there is no business left.

There is no better example than the *quality of the product or service*. This will be the result of your own procedures from initial design through to implementation and subsequent production standards. It is not a sign of efficiency, however, if the product or service is over-specified for its purpose. This may merely be throwing money away that you either lose from profit or the customer pays for in the price until somebody else steals the opportunity to economize and compete more effectively.

There are many other pointers which either stare you in the face, can be deduced from available statistical information or can be found upon research and enquiry. Those that we are concerned with here can all be regarded as prerequisites to financial success, the interpretation of which we discuss later.

If we are to be successful in marketing we will need to be consistent in our market research and prognosis. The information gathered must be relevant and unbiased, and the questions addressed effectively and to the point. Advertising campaigns will be the more efficient in terms of business won if they are equally consistent and well thought out. It is usually wise to concentrate on the best features of your product that your research tells you are of value to the prospective customers. You will probably concentrate your resources on one theme, frequently repeating this so that the message gets home. It is often a sign of inefficient advertising if it is always varied, haphazard and short in duration.

Margins will be protected so long as cost inflation can be passed on at manageable intervals in price increases. If you do not do so, and are not able to compensate elsewhere in the product specification or otherwise then you do not have an efficient enterprise.

How many firms get into dispute because their terms and conditions of business are lacking in certain areas or ambiguous? There is a host of matters ranging from the performance of the goods through to the terms upon which payment must be made. There are many good examples around and your solicitor will have an omnibus edition on his word processor which you may condense to those most relevant to you.

It is clearly a measure of efficiency if your scrap and wastage levels are low. They are not the same, and require a different approach. Wastage may come, for example, from cutting circular shapes from square sheets of metal, or from evaporation of liquids. It is inherent in the process and may be overcome by developing the process. Scrap, on the other hand, is the result of some human, mechanical or other error in the course of production. An efficient system will flag it up at the earliest possible stage before further costs are added to a non-saleable product. Such a system will lead to immediate steps to eradicate the root cause wherever possible.

Either way they can both represent an enormous cost. If they should, for instance, be as high as 10 per cent of sales then they may well be equal to or greater than the profit earned.

Put it to the test by analysing your returns and complaints by quantity, reason and value. How many customers are you upsetting and what is this costing you in forgone profits? What would your profit have been last month in the absence of these returns? You will need to go beyond measuring the damage if it is at all material and focus on removing the cause.

It is a sign of poor efficiency if your plant and machinery is always breaking down, the first suspicion being pointed at the adequacy of the preventive maintenance programmes.

You should be skilful at balancing production with orders received so that you neither overstock nor run out of product. The same goes for the requisition of raw materials, components and finished products. Matched to this is the need to know where exactly in the stores the various goods are since if you cannot find them they are of no earthly use.

Goods and materials are often 'left in a corner' even after the last production run has been signalled. This way they can become automatic candidates for obsolescence. A high obsolescence level is an indication of somebody's poor judgement.

During stock checks any differences between physical stock and book stock will be written off. If these are high or worse, unrecorded, then something is wrong. If you do not know what finished stocks you have you are in a worse plight. They will be occupying space and will eventually become obsolete when they could have been sold.

Just the physical appearance of the shop floor and offices will tell much about the standards you can expect elsewhere. A cleanly swept shop with clear gangways, neatly stacked goods and an absence of paperwork collecting dust on surfaces speaks much for the business.

Space wasted with obsolete standing plant, goods and raw materials is not only expensive in terms of wasted rates and other occupation costs; it also leads to an inefficient plant layout and slows down the production flow.

The efficiency within offices will be measured in terms of the number of documents handled per person, the debtor collection record and bad debts, breaches of overdraft facilities, the record of being placed on 'stop lists' and many more.

Under-insurance through lack of care and organization can leave you in desperate straits. It is essential that somebody experienced in the subject reads the small print through carefully. Regular meetings with insurers and brokers should be conducted on a 'what if' basis, and they should expose weaknesses.

Ageing is another indicator which runs right through the whole organization and may affect:

- The average management age – no new blood
- An ageing and less efficient plant facility

- Premises
- Product profile – no new products for years
- An outmoded attitude to employees
- Obsolete office equipment and computers
- Over-used advertising or marketing procedures

Apply the ageing test to all the areas of the business that you think are relevant and determine whether this process is affecting the general efficiency of the company.

It will certainly not be considered efficient if your total costs of operation are excessive. If you have indulged in expensive, prestigious premises and facilities before your business is off the ground, or are carrying too high a proportion of fixed overheads, this will justifiably be seen as a weakness.

The converse argument is that the absence of suitable premises may check your growth prospects. This is a dangerous area and you must balance the future need and benefits with your cost structure now. An additional factory or set of offices never comes alone. There is always the strong temptation to fill them with people, not to mention the step up in occupancy costs of all kinds.

The use of subcontractors can be a necessary and desirable practice or a sign of inefficiency. It is never, for example, wise to build up internal facilities to cover short-term peaks. These are best shunted outside or you will be left financing the facilities long afterwards.

If on the other hand you have to resort to subcontractors because you have failed to meet deadlines you run the risk of goods arriving from your own and outside sources at the same time.

One of the worst signs of weakness is that of launching new products when you are not fully prepared. You should ensure that you first have your factory pipe-line or handling centre fully ready to handle orders or the repercussions could be disastrous. It must also be ready to deal with returns which could be considerable in the early stages, and it must be capable of responding to changes in anticipated requirements such as the colour or product mix.

However well prepared you are with pre-launch stocks, it is a mistake to launch the product immediately prior to a holiday shutdown. You cannot risk being let down by incorrectly balanced stocks or facilities which deny a swift response to changing requirements.

Another common error is to earmark *all* production or deliveries for priority sale. There have to be times when you are able to balance your shelf stocks or otherwise recover your shortages. Everything cannot be priority at the same time.

It can be an expensive mistake to improve leasehold property without first obtaining the landlord's permission and a surveyor's report on the state of the premises before and after the action. Failure to do so is inefficient. The improvements will be used against you at rent review time without any recourse. You will want to ensure that these tenants' improvements are properly documented so that they do not impose a further future burden on you beyond their initial cost.

These are some of the criteria by which you and outsiders may judge the general level of efficiency. They all have a profound effect upon financial results. Other areas are discussed below.

Risk status

Consider whether your activity is the subject of any special risks. Businesses in such areas draw additional profits in compensation and outsiders will be conscious of these risks when they decide whether to invest or advance finance. They will be more inclined to do so if you are indeed reaping rewards commensurate with conducting business in these conditions.

You may be subjecting yourselves to unnecessary risks by not taking avoiding action. Take the possibility of fire. Do you store dangerous combustible items away from the main centre and do you take the other standard precautions? Suppose these do not work – would you be able to maintain your business through other arrangements to bring the goods in or subcontract them elsewhere?

There is a whole science based upon the elimination or mitigation of risks by appropriate attention before they arise. It is risk management. This is very much in your interests and those of your insurers that have to meet the costs of failure.

You should scan every one of your business activities from a risk point of view. Ask yourself all the things that could conceivably go wrong, and then think of the best means of avoiding them or dealing with the consequences. If you want some examples and advice tap into the industry through the specialists direct or through your insurers.

What about other risks which result neither from your choice of industry nor your practical circumstances? There are risks of another kind that can quite easily be self-inflicted. They have to do with the degree to which you take care to spread your exposure, for example: you may have only a small number of large customers. Some businesses seize an opportunity to serve one major operation and expand rapidly with them, until they pull the plug, when the whole business goes down.

Suppliers to the motor industry may, for example, find that the customer takes the work in-house at short notice. Alternatively, they may go into liquidation and they take a host of component suppliers down with them. Then again, their owners may relocate the business to an alternative overseas plant and require the component suppliers to be close at hand. At best you may have the opportunity to reinvest in that new location, assuming you are given the chance.

You could be working as a concession within a single store group and fall victim to its policy to refurbish or sell off the freeholds in which you trade. What can you do if the landlord increases the rent or changes the other trading terms to your disadvantage? Such arrangements are often renewed on short terms.

It is very easy to get yourself into a position where a single supplier can go out of business, withdraw from the product or blackmail you on price.

What if your computer department goes on strike? Suppose your design subcontractor suddenly dies? It is a good sign if you can spread all the risks in this category so that no single withdrawal of custom, supply or service will cause an injury that you cannot ride. The first requirement is that you be actively conscious of the problem. You should apply the principle to all areas of the business to ascertain which are more or less 'risk efficient'. Then consider avoiding action or steps that can be taken over time to soften the blow.

Competitiveness

An efficient firm is one that has reduced its unit costs to a point where it can fix a price that will produce sound profits yet keep competitors out.

The product or service will be seen as good value for money and not be unnecessarily over-specified. It will be fit for its purpose, reliable and of an appropriate appearance.

Enterprising firms know that a market or brand leader that excels all others in the field is likely to be longer lasting and will remain competitive. In order to keep their product or service in this exalted position they are willing to invest large sums in the most recent technology and manufacturing methods.

There are fewer things through which a business is judged than its ability to keep its delivery promises. If for any reason you are likely to fail your customer in this respect then he will be more willing to forgive you if you give him advance notice as soon as you know yourself. It is not a sign of an efficient business if you knowingly quote over-optimistic delivery dates in a bid to win an order. This may work once or twice but the word will get around and the orders will dry up.

Finally, you should be creating an image in which you are seen as the concern that does not stand still with time. Your customers will lose confidence in you if you do not convince them that you are abreast with new developments in your product field. You will want them to be confident that your product cannot be bettered elsewhere.

To summarize, the main criteria by which competitiveness may be judged are:

- Quality
- Price
- Delivery
- Innovation and new products

The emphasis is likely to be on any one or a combination of these and the price may be the last in the ranking order.

As tariff barriers fall and the wider European market becomes more free you will be facing it with confidence or with apprehension. This will be the acid test. Do you stand up well?

Market intelligence

It is usually essential to know what is going on elsewhere in the market. You need to know what new developments to products and services are afoot, who is building up manufacturing capacities, who is making special pricing bargains, who is approaching your customers and a multitude besides.

Start research by trying to determine the size of the market in which you operate and your market share. Then you will want to know the size of the other main players that affect you.

Next will come a thorough review of your product strengths and weaknesses in contrast to your competitors. Exactly how do you each differ? You will ask yourself what you have that others do not. If you do not know this you will hardly be in a position to make any special claims in your advertising or dialogue with potential converts.

We hear a lot about industrial espionage. How much it exists nobody really knows. What is, however, very commonplace is the extent to which commercial secrets are carelessly bandied around by comparative juniors in the organization.

Potential take-overs are immediately recognized by the unfamiliar executive car parked outside the boardroom, the shop floor often being the first to know. Dangerous rumours often start this way but it is surprising how often comparatively junior people are on the ball. A few hints put together, substantiated by subsequent developments, will make a theory sound very rational indeed.

In the same way, travelling sales representatives and service personnel soon pick up market intelligence. Your switchboard operator will be both a source and a high risk area in this sense. No matter how well you brief the operator this is the first point of contact with the company, and there are many who are skilled in learning just what they want from this source.

And then of course people change jobs and bring their source information with them.

Tittle-tattle aside, the need to know much about the market and developments in it is a very serious business that you ignore at your peril. A healthy operation is one that does not go about its business oblivious to what is happening around it.

You have to obtain knowledge of the actions of your competitors and feedback from your customers. Marketing personnel, service engineers, sales representatives and other visitors are all good sources of information which go towards supplementing formally conducted market research.

Executives in the same industry often have good rapport and understanding. They will discuss developments and exchange opinions on new products and selling techniques. There is a danger that these discussions can become altogether too cosy. You are not conducting effective market research if you question your competitors. It is your customer and the end user you should be approaching.

It is often a waste of time to send sales representatives out knocking on doors, or cold canvassing as it is called. It is far better to make an appointment first. Even before this, check with the head office that the branch is authorized to place orders, but remember you can cultivate branch enthusiasm to your advantage at the centre.

The drawing office can often be a surprising but very useful marketing route. They will often be able to obtain admission to customers' official parts lists, this being necessary to ensure that your own product is consistent. The detail may present you with marketing opportunities. Your buying department may also benefit from the information in ensuring consistency with the product you are already providing and any bought out parts.

Be wise to the opportunities that the world markets present to you. For example, you may have a product that sells well in the summer season. If so, find some other product to fill the gap in the winter, or better still, explore the prospects of selling in the other hemisphere in your own winter time.

You may spot differential pricing on goods entering the country, possibly through dumping practices of companies looking for extra marginal returns (having first met their basic requirements in the home market).

Does this present you with re-export sales opportunities elsewhere?

Corporate image

Not every firm needs to develop its corporate image. The essential ingredients of developed corporate images are often packaged by marketing firms at enormous expense (when you consider that they are mostly repeat sales of the same commodity). What you pay for is the time invested by experts and the risk to which they expose themselves through those that do not proceed with an order.

A good corporate image for major operations, particularly those selling branded goods to a large market, is essential.

The first step will be to assess your strengths and weaknesses and the claims that you can make about your product or service. Then some applied market research will winkle out which of those is important to the customer so that you know where to place the emphasis.

The immediate signs by which a business can be recognized are:

- Its name
- Its symbol (eg, its shorthand name or logo)
- Its adopted colours (livery)
- Slogans used repetitively
- Advertising style
- Uniformity of product appearance or wrapping
- Uniformity of letterhead design
- External or charitable activities with which it is associated
- The standard of its reception, showrooms, offices and factories.

The idea is to place consistent emphasis on these features which, taken together, all add up to the particular corporate image with which we associate the company.

The usual starting point is the company name, the symbol, the adopted colour recognition scheme and peripherals such as letter heads, invoice designs and order pads.

Well designed letterheads may not sound essential to you, but we all know what an excellent impression they can convey to us before we even see the company or its product.

Then you begin to put the meat on the bone with such matters as slogans, product wrapping and other matters that add to your identification.

Think what a good impression it creates if you can show new customers around an eye catching in-house exhibition of your product, or if you can conduct them through clean, efficient-looking and well organized offices and factory facilities.

The aim will be to develop each area referred to so that the company behind the product will be instantly recognized on the occasion of each purchase. The purpose is to develop product loyalty and company goodwill. It is hoped that this will cement the customer preference to the company's products that exist now and which may be introduced in the future.

There is no doubt that this works extremely well in many established cases. Whether it does or not, it will still be seen to be modern in outlook and a real (but sometimes imagined) sign of good health.

There is nothing to stop you from giving thought to each of the elements that make up the corporate image which are listed above. You can start to develop your own in each of these areas, with or without professional advice, according to your circumstances.

Management and Pareto

Pareto was responsible for some profound observations.

The most important relevant to business teaches us that we can often hit 80 per cent of the problem with 20 per cent of the effort if it is properly directed. It is often the case that 80 per cent of the orders or profits come from 20 per cent of the customers or products. This warrants close attention to recognizing priorities and maximizing returns.

A company may have many sound products or profit centres which it fails to develop because all its time is dragged into dealing with the single problem child. The same analogy can be drawn in many other situations which apply to the business. They may have to do with administrative matters or a multitude of items concerned with the way in which the business is conducted.

The optimum application of this principle will rebound with certainty on the health of the business. It requires that you should look at it with fresh eyes to ascertain whether you or any of the management have been drawn into this common malaise. Sometimes it takes the experience and independence of a complete outsider to recognize the symptoms and the problem areas. You should be careful that the wrong opinions are not first formed by those financing you because they will be well aware of its manifestations.

Availability of finance

A healthy business will have its bankers and other institutions putting pressure on it to take out another line of finance.

It will be able to play off one against another to an extent without damaging relationships and will achieve the best possible terms.

Lines of credit will be already available although not in use. No commitment fee will be paid for these on-tap facilities and some of them will be rotated in use from time to time so that there is less temptation for them to be withdrawn.

Alternative business plans will show the possible range of finance that may be required to fit most circumstances, and you will not be left wanting should an emergency arise. This may come in the form of a fall off in business, an unprofitable period or in times of investment or expansion.

This will be within the self-imposed and external constraints regarding gearing, and these will be discussed later under 'Liquidity'.

Nothing can be more crucial than the availability of finance when it is needed most. Lack of regard to this area is quite the worst of all signs of ill-health. It should certainly not put the brakes on prospects of sound growth.

Business controls

Management control information

Understanding all the signs of a healthy business, and applying them to your own, will do much to ensure that it stays on the rails.

However, some form of quantitative business control information is necessary to enable you to measure the results of your endeavours. These are also invaluable in the day-to-day running of the operation.

The basic need is to receive control information at regular intervals for matters of particular consequence that can go wrong in the short term. This may include frequent reports on the quality of the products in the manufacturing line, the level of wastage or scrap being incurred or the rate of progress on a major contract. Such information is usually provided in statistical form rather than financial, and promotes immediate action in the specific area with which it is concerned.

The next line of control information may be available on a weekly basis. This may include feedback on which products are selling best and to which customers. It may form the spur for follow-up checks by sales representatives or telephone enquiries. Weekly payroll analysis may be another and many more examples will come to mind.

This will then be followed by the financial overview contained in the monthly management accounts. The monthly circulation of this kind of information is just right because it allows for a substantial enough level of feedback to be digested and acted upon, commensurate with the practical considerations involved in its preparation.

It goes without saying that information on profitability must be available as soon as possible after the period analysed and at sufficiently regular intervals. This should be prepared to show results by department and cost centre for the managers specifically responsible. The accounts will include an analysis showing the product or product group margins being earned. They will include more general statements summarizing the results, cash flow, and the balance sheet (or capital employed) information.

They will all be compared with plan and the best disciplined concerns will also show current forecasts. These will of course show line by line figures of all labour, material and overhead items in the most appropriate form to meet the firm's needs at all levels.

Analyses prepared monthly, but supplementary to the main accounts, may give details of purchases of each item or component by supplier, quantity, and cost.

Controls by exception

Before we proceed further it is important to state one essential principle. Management is never concerned to know of all the things that are going right. It needs to know what is going wrong and what exactly has to be addressed.

So far as possible therefore control forms should highlight or summarize – *by exception*.

That is to say that they should flag the divergences from plan or predetermined standard so that priority can be addressed to them directly. Information produced necessarily in comprehensive form often presents itself as a daunting sea of figures to the reader, but there is nothing to stop those responsible for its preparation from compiling a simple summary of the most salient points.

The principle in submitting control figures is the same as that which should be followed in meetings. You do not spend all your time discussing matters that are proceeding well because you will want to get down to the task of dealing with those that are not. So you should remember this when presenting the facts that will be considered there.

The exceptions should be reported separately from any general statements.

Control information formats

On page 37 there is an example of a simple form used for the regular review of the employment status, and an example of one used for the review of various work tasks will be found on page 43.

A number of further business control forms are recommended in this chapter. They are by no means exhaustive but have been selected to include all the information that is most critical to any business.

Their use should be sufficient in most cases to ensure that you have your finger on the pulse for day-to-day control. Since we are here concerned with the control of the business as it is conducted on a day-to-day basis, forms used in formal forward business plans will be found in this chapter.

We now consider the following useful control forms:

- Key statistics summary
- Reconciliation of actual and budget profit
- Capital employed statement
- Profit and loss statement
- Conversion rate

- Liquidity summary
- Working capital control
- Capital expenditure and value analysis programme
- Project rolling forecast
- Capital expenditure authorization
- Capital expenditure appraisal working paper

Key statistics summary

The object of this form is to bring all the most critical information on to one single sheet that tells the whole story (see page 60).

It contains the order book situation so you know if orders are being taken or drying up. It then shows the 'big' important figures such as sales, total overhead, profit, capital employed, capital commitments, cash balances and headroom, and employee status.

Trade discounts are highlighted from which you can ensure that your margins are not being diluted by 'soft' selling methods.

Crucial ratios are included (details of which will be discussed later in the text).

The analysis of credit notes will enable you to keep your eye on problem areas and their severity. It is also used to summarize the performance on margins by product or product group. Little of any importance has been omitted.

Reconciliation of actual and budget profit

This form (on page 61) is an excellent example of reporting by exception. It starts off with the budgeted profit and shows, by value and major reason, the divergences from plan (good and bad) which will have resulted in the actual profit earned.

Its objective, therefore, is to serve as a summary of the main highlights of performance in the period. It will include all the normal categories of variance which tell the story, saving the reader from sifting through a sea of figures for himself.

KEY STATISTICS SUMMARY

Company .... Date ....

As at		Budget	Actual	Previous year
Order book Orders on hand – previous period Orders received in period Sales invoiced in period		(£000)	(£000)	(£000)
Orders on hand				
Cumulative figures: Sales Orders Discounts given Total overhead Net profit				
Net profit forecast for year Capital employed Capital commitments Sales per employee Added value per employee				
Cash balance Cash flow Cash headroom				
Credit notes by major reason: (list)				
Direct employees Indirect employees Total employees		No	No	No
Ratios Debtor days Creditor days Stock and WIP months Interest cover Unresolved debtor queries Solvency test score				
Return on capital employed Net profit on sales Gearing		%	%	%
Gross margin/added value by product group: (list)				

RECONCILIATION OF ACTUAL AND BUDGET PROFIT

Please state whether month or cumulative: ....
(£000)

Budget profit

Reconciling items:

Actual profit

Capital employed statement

This form (see page 62) is unbelievably useful. It shows on a single sheet the assets employed in the business, how they are funded, profits earned, cash generated and the return on capital employed. It can be used for regular monthly reports and also for planning and forecasting purposes.

The figures for the opening balance sheet will normally be entered in the first column followed by the current period, and finally the forecast for the end of the year. By deducting one column from another, the movement for the current period – year to date or the forecast for the year – can be entered in the final two columns. These, in effect, are equivalent to a cash flow statement, the movement on the profit and loss account being the trading result.

The foot of the form allows for the calculation of the return on capital employed which will be discussed again later.

CAPITAL EMPLOYED STATEMENT

Trading unit ....   Date ....

Currency ....

	Previous	Current	Forecast	Movement in funds	
	....	....	....	Current period	Year to date
	(000)	(000)	(000)	(000)	(000)
Fixed assets					
Cost					
Depreciation					
Net book value (1)					
Current assets					
Cash					
Trade debtors					
Inter-company debtors					
Sundry debtors					
Stocks					
Less:					
Current liabilities					
Trade creditors					
Inter-company creditors					
Sundry creditors					
Taxation					
Net working capital (4)					
Total capital employed (1+4)					

continued over

Financed by:					
Inter-company loans					
Bank overdraft					
Acceptance credits					
Loans					
Capital and reserves					
Profit and loss account					
Result					
Add back interest					
Total profit before interest					
Return on total capital employed – (% pa)				%	%

Notes: 1. Basis – average capital employed – historic with no adjustments
profits – before tax and interest

Profit and loss statement

The format shown on page 64 contains the rudiments for all the profit and loss information such as the detailed analysis of department overheads as well as the summary front sheet reproduced.

The number of columns used is very much a matter of choice, but space is always the limiting factor, together with the need to make the document readable.

In the example shown, the columns on the left of the narrative allow you to read actual performance against budget for the current period and the year to date. Had there been more room these might have included columns for the main variances between budget and actual performance. However, these can be read at a glance and require further interpretation in any event. Percentages of sales may also be included, save for the need to pare back the number of figures to be read. These can soon be

PROFIT AND LOSS STATEMENT

	Month		Cumulative		Full year		
	Budget	Actual	Budget	Actual	Prior actual	Budget	Forecast
Sales							
Product A							
Product B							
Product C							
Direct costs							
Material							
Labour							
Other							
Contribution							
Overheads							
Research and development							
Occupancy							
Fixed production costs							
Administration							
Selling and marketing							
Financial							
Interest							
Net profit							

calculated and will be used towards the main reconciliation statement discussed above.

To the right of the narrative the figures represent a full year. Firstly, those relating to the full previous year serve as a good base to know from where you started. Then comes the budget showing your aspirations for the current year. The final column is used to show the current best estimate of the result for the present year. It will be based upon your actual experience to date (column 4) added to which will be the benefit of all that you know is happening or about to happen before the year ends. In short, the right-hand columns are used to show the progression from prior experience to aspiration to current expectancy.

Some companies would include a column in this section to show the annual moving total. This is used to show trends. Some would use it to forecast beyond the end of the current financial year so that they are always thinking some distance ahead.

If room permitted you might include a column to show the change in the forecast from month to month. Such changes can only be the result of topical matters (unless they reflect errors of accounting or judgement) and this can be a useful way of highlighting matters of immediate interest. These can otherwise be deduced by comparison with the statement for the previous month.

Allowing for space restrictions, therefore, the format shown is probably the most useful and covers all the important principles.

Conversion rate
When you have grasped all the foregoing performance statements you will want to know whether or not you are adding successfully to your store of orders in hand (that is unless you sell over the counter when an order book is not relevant).

The conversion rate form (see page 66) enables you to plot progress in absolute terms. It also enables you to review whether or not you are getting your fair share of conversion of orders from quotations submitted. If this is poor by industry standards you will wish to investigate. If it is more than excellent you may wish to ensure that you are maximizing your prices and not taking on huge volumes of unprofitable work.

Conversion Rate – Product A

	Previous month		Previous quarter		Year to date	
	Number	Value	Number	Value	Number	Value
Enquiries						
Quotations submitted						
Resultant orders						
Conversion rate	%	%	%	%	%	%

It is useful to prepare a separate statement for each product or product group, differentiating if possible by the level of margin.

Working capital control

This is a working document (see page 68) which can be used to highlight where in the business cash is being unnecessarily absorbed.

After entering the date of review (which will depend in each case on the availability of information) the actual monetary value of each item is shown in the next column. From this the actual ratio of calendar days' or months' holdings is calculated, and stated next against the target days or months that have been predetermined. The method of calculating these is discussed later.

By dividing the actual monetary value by the actual ratio and multiplying it by the target ratio you will be able to enter the target value in the penultimate column.

The difference between target and actual monetary values, line by line, will show where cash is unnecessarily locked up in the capital employed. Only enter the areas in the final column where you are deficient. The total of these will reveal by just how much cash resources can be improved if action can be taken to hit all target performances in this critical area. Success here will automatically increase cash headroom.

Liquidity Summary

(000)

	Current month	Cumulative	Next month forecast	Year forecast
Source				
Profit Depreciation				
Application				
Capital expenditure Debtors +/− Stocks +/− Creditors +/− Tax				
Cash flow movement				
Opening balance				
Fresh finance Loan repayments				
Closing balance				
Total facilities				
Headroom				

Liquidity summary

The importance of liquidity will be reinforced time and again.

This form (above) shows midway whether or not a positive cash flow is being generated from the business. The lower half goes on to compare the resultant total facilities available with the funds consumed within the business. This is the measure of cash headroom which is carried forward to be highlighted on the front key statistics summary.

Working Capital Control

Category	Date of review	Value (000)	Ratio		Target value (000)	Potential gain (000)
			Actual	Target		

Raw materials
  Steel
  Brass
  Copper						

Work-in-progress
  Product A
  Product B
  Product C						

Finished stocks
  Product A
  Product B
  Product C						

Debtors
  Home
  Export						

Creditors						

Notes: Debtor and creditor ratios will be expressed in calendar days; other categories will be shown in months to one decimal point

Capital expenditure and value analysis programme

All well-disciplined businesses maximize their returns by the use of informed techniques of project assessment before they commit the investment. The project may involve new capital expenditure or changes involving smaller outlays to improve the returns on existing projects. By this we mean the type that involves the use of value analysis techniques.

It is not just a case of deciding whether or not the potential returns from a project warrant a green or a red light. Common sense has it that you will have the greatest prospect of success if you select the most profitable projects first to occupy your time and resources.

The best way of ensuring that this principle is followed is to use the particular form offered for this purpose. It contains columns to plan and control progress, and is ideal for discussion at meetings.

Capital Expenditure and Value Analysis Programme

Project ranking list

Adopted projects		Time to complete (weeks)			Investment risk	Anticipated return		Comments and
Priority ranking	Title	R&D	Prototype	Pre-production	(£000)	Present value at 30%	DCF%	progress reviews
1								
2								
3								
4								
5								
6								
7								
8								
9								
10								
11								
12								
13								
14								
15								
16								
17								
18								
19								
20								

It also serves as a checklist to ensure that decisions taken are indeed being followed through.

The investment risk column will remind you how much capital is at risk on each project. The anticipated return is first measured at a minimum cut-off rate (30 per cent in the illustration) and then the overall discounted rate of return is shown for those using this recommended technique.

Some prefer to use the measure of pay-back by calculating when their initial outlay will be returned in the form of profits on the project.

Once you have this information it is not a simple matter of giving highest priority to the projects that score the most in terms of present value, rate of return or payback. Risk has to be considered, general strategies and all kinds of practical issues.

When the business has taken all into account, and decided the priority order of ranking, this should be strictly followed until circumstances change or all agree that there is good and sound reason for revising the original plan.

The form provides the basis with which all these matters can be determined and goes beyond the simple test applied to any individual project. It represents a very useful business control.

Project rolling forecast

This form (opposite) allows you to follow the progress once expenditure on a project has commenced. It will tell you whether or not the total capital authorized for the purpose is likely to fall short of or exceed authorized limits.

It may also be used for revenue projects of all kinds, and has particular relevance in the construction industry. It will be prepared monthly as a regular review source.

Capital expenditure authorization form

This is the kind of form that is used to present a case to the authorizing executive, management meeting or board, for approval. Most of the information contained within it is self-explanatory (see page 72). Its purpose is to bring together all relevant figures and arguments in support of the proposal. Most advanced companies have their own variation on the central theme.

Project Rolling Forecast

Company/plant ....
Asset category ....

Date ....
Currency (000) ....

Project title	No.	Current year				Cumulative			
		Budget	Authorized	Cost to date	Forecast	Budget	Authorized	Cost to date	Forecast
Totals									

Notes:-
1. The cumulative columns should only be completed for projects lasting more than one year.
2. Please indicate separately those items carried forward from the budget of the previous year.
3. All capital items should be included where expenditure is likely in the year whether or not they were submitted for consideration in the original capital budget.
4. Separate evaluation and capital expenditure forms must be submitted for each project in accordance with the standard authorization procedures before commencing.
5. Please use separate sheets by asset category for machinery and motor vehicles, and as otherwise convenient.
6. Please use continuation sheets where necessary taking the totals to the final page.

Capital Expenditure Authorization Form

		Office use	
Company Dept		Full board	Yes/No
Completion date		Capital budget no.	....
Submitted by		Budget gain(+)loss(−)	£
(Signature) (Signature)		Number allocated	....
Approved Date		Coding	
(Signature)		Capital account	
		Revenue account	

Basic Information and Cost		£
Brief description		—
Purchase price or mfg cost		
Installation cost or other initial outlay		
	(please specify)	
Grant, (if any)		( )
Assets being replaced (if any)		—
Book value at replacement	£	( )
Estimated disposal value		
Additional working capital (if applicable)		
Total net investment and cash requirement		

Economic case

Addition	Expansion	Replacement	Welfare
(Please delete as appropriate)			

Report:

(Please specify brief notes covering the reason for the expenditure and the benefits or savings anticipated, highlighting any spare capacity or bottlenecks caused or relieved through this project)

Cases Fully Appraised		
	Pay back period	years
	DCF overall %	%
	Present value at %	£
	Ultimate cost	£
	For post appraisal on	

Capital Expenditure Appraisal Working Paper (side 1)

Company ....

Project title:	Capital budget number:

Basic Information and Cost	£
Brief description	
Purchase price or mfg cost	
Installation cost or other initial outlay	
	Please specify
Grant, (if any)	( )
Assets being replaced (if any)	
Book value at replacement	£
Estimated disposal value	( )
Additional working capital (if applicable)	
Total net investment and cash requirement	

Cash Flows

Year	Net cash flow	PV@ %	PV@ %
0			
1			
2			
3			
4			
5			
6			
7			
8			
9			
10			

Capital expenditure appraisal working paper

This is a working document and not one of the type that is usually circulated as a business control form.

Any number and variety of discounted cash flow calculations can be prepared in the columns provided for those familiar with this discipline. The general justification box which is ticked will dictate how the columns are used in practice.

(side 2)

Product Information – Additional Volume

Unit Details	£	Year	Qty	Price (ea)	Total billing	Contribution @___%
Gross selling price		1				
Less discount _____ % _____						
Less royalty _____ % _____		2				
Net selling price		3				
Direct/works cost _____		4				
Contribution per unit _____		5				
		6				

General Justification | Tick

Increased activity of current products and services	
Expansion of range of products and services	
Essential replacement – asset(s) in total state of disrepair	
Excessive repair and running costs rendering asset(s) uneconomical	
Improved features on new asset(s) giving rise to improved quality	
Improved features on new asset(s) giving rise to extra capacity	
Standardization of product range	
Any other (please specify)	

Notes on basis of valuation (including savings)

As such it contains the basic assumptions and facts that lie in detail behind the authorization form discussed immediately above. Some managers can make good use of the form themselves, and others who are sufficiently numerate may wish to use it to familiarize themselves with the underlying assumptions and express their own view on their validity.

Summary

No daily or weekly scrap report forms have been included above and a number of others could have been added. An example might be the value of purchases of each material or product by supplier on a current and yearly basis.

Each business will have devised its own forms designed to catch the most vital and relevant information.

However, the examples shown will incorporate all that is vital to any business. They may be refined, and more detail may be added on separate control forms to support some of the summary information used.

You can of course go on for ever and sometimes the volume of paperwork and time taken stands in the way of progress. On occasions a glance with the human eye will reveal much more than a million forms, and you have to develop a sense of proportion.

If you can use a computer to call off most of the information from a single data source the production effort can be much reduced. In accounting parlance, an enormous amount can be done working from an 'extended trial balance' as one of the main base sources of information. At a flick of a switch all the information is produced once the initial system is set up.

If you employ each of the above examples as a minimum, you will certainly have reached a high standard of excellence in the use of business control forms. Remember that in the absence of appropriate business control forms you cannot hope to have your finger on the pulse.

Financial appraisal – the business results

The meaning of financial efficiency

The financial wing

The financial wing of a business may be measured for its effectiveness just like any other department. The following will give an appreciation of what we mean by financial efficiency within that department.

First, it will be the prompt provider of most, if not all, of the control information that management use to interpret performance and address problem areas. These will be comprehensive but highlight the vital areas and departures from plan in a manner that is easy to follow. A myriad figures staring up at you from a single report form can be daunting to say the least.

In a good system the detail will be shown on backing analysis sheets while the most critical information will be shown in summary form where it is most accessible – at the front.

The disciplines of planning and forecasting will be well established. Changes in the forecasts from month to month will reflect topical matters with which management will identify, and contain no unflagged surprises. Having said that, there is no virtue in suppressing bad news once it surfaces for whatever reason. Some organizations do so until an appropriate opportunity occurs to give (delayed) 'advance warning alerts'. These soften the blow, after which the matter is incorporated in the figures. To adhere to a strict 'no surprises' doctrine requires much smoothing and interference with figures, to the point of suppressing information. The result is not a dynamic feedback of information which enables management to read what is happening and act at the earliest moment. It is not to be recommended.

Movements in working capital will be monitored and explained using the means that we will discuss further in this chapter.

A debtor ageing list will be regularly produced and acted upon. There will be a means of control at the point of accepting orders for those debtors that are a regular or potential problem. If this infers cash only trading the correct procedures will be in place to ensure that credit is not given.

Day-to-day cash flow controls will be sound and changes in liquidity requirements will be foreseen and negotiated in advance. It is paradoxical that cash raised from shareholders by rights issues will be ruled out unless it can first be demonstrated that forward liquidity by other means is secure. This will show how important it is to be very well prepared in this area.

Good negotiating skills are essential because there are many areas which are technically and financially orientated and come under that discipline. Examples may be the terms of borrowing, the rates of interest paid, taxation, acquisitions and disposals, commercial contracts, legal matters and many more.

The financial wing may be restricted to offering advice on these matters or take the front line negotiating position or sole responsibility.

It will also need to exercise good judgement in its own area of control and play a useful and active role in its contribution to the general management of the enterprise.

The department will need to be efficient in all areas under its control. It will, for example, ensure that a proper plant register exists and that it is cross-referenced to identification numbers and the physical location plan. This in turn will be linked to the insurance register which will be up to date as to its content and values in the event of a catastrophe.

An efficient concern will have a forward business plan which covers the next three years (some go to five) and shows the effect of major variations that might be encountered. It will show how sensitive the business plan is to changes in the areas most subject to variation.

There will be full financial analysis of all significant proposals for capital expenditure. Nothing has a more profound effect on the future well-being of the business.

The financial wing acts as the custodian of all the assets and liabilities employed in each operation, often amounting to millions of pounds in any business once established. The manner in which it carries out those responsibilities is central to the well-being of the concern.

The interpretation of financial output

Until now we have discussed *how* a business stays healthy and profitable. We have considered which disciplines and controls are most likely to lead to success, given the external environment in which it operates. There are of course many factors that go towards creating a profitable business, and it must be conceded that luck also plays some part.

The foregoing chapters, therefore, may encapsulate the factors which will go towards making or preserving a healthy operation. While their presence may be indicative of a successful enterprise, they do not in themselves provide a means of actual measurement.

It is the output of the financial wing that management and outsiders alike use to *measure* how successfully this aim has been achieved.

It is to these that we now turn in order to measure specifically how we stand.

Standards of measurement

Leaving the general principles of business well-being for a while we turn to the more clinical means of measurement which can collectively be regarded as the financial performance standards.

Financial institutions and other outsiders will use these to judge us even more than we do ourselves. They act as common denominators and fill many gaps in information about the operation which are not generally available to external bodies. Unfortunately, there are so many as to be bewildering. Some are relevant to one purpose but not to another, and it all depends on whether you are looking at the entity as a shareholder, banker, financier, employee, member of the public or potential investor.

They mainly consist of ratios and relative percentages. An improvement in one will often have a spin-off effect on others. It will pay to keep this feature of interrelationship in mind as we progress. A number of them are mathematically correlated so that when you know a change in one you can calculate the effect on the other if you are sufficiently practised.

It will help at the outset if we divide them into separate categories or classifications. As each of these is discussed we will judge their merits and particular usage:

- Shareholder returns and risk
    Dividend per share and yield
    Earnings per share and dividend cover
    Price/earnings ratio
    Asset cover
    Cash flow per share
- Banking ratios
    Interest cover
    Leverage
    Break-up value
- Asset turnover ratios
    Fixed asset to sales
    Total assets to sales
    Debtors and debtor days
    Creditors and creditor days
    Stock turnover

- Profitability
  - Contribution or gross margin
  - Fixed overhead proportion
  - Profit percentage on sales
  - Profit growth, organic and purchased
  - Return on capital employed
- Commercial
  - Market share
  - Home sales/export
  - Sales per employee/profit per employee
  - Average remuneration
- Liquidity
  - Quick ratio
  - Current ratio
  - Gearing
  - Cash headroom
  - Ageing of external facilities
  - Capacity to borrow and security
- Solvency tests
  - The ultimate guide?
- Statutory disclosures

In the following pages are many examples of how these standards of measurement are calculated and how they apply. It will be simpler to follow if all the references to figures are drawn from a single specimen profit statement and a single specimen capital employed statement. These are set out below. The figures are in thousands (of whichever currency) but as many noughts may be added or subtracted as you wish. The principles remain the same.

Specimen profit statement	(000)	%
Sales		
Home	1,477	74
Export	530	26
	2,007	100
Direct cost of sales		
Materials	702	35
Direct labour	361	18
Other variable costs	120	6
	1,183	59
Contribution (gross margin)	824	41
Fixed costs		
Factory or warehouse	121	6
Depreciation	140	7
Administrative	120	6
Selling and marketing	100	5
Distribution	60	3
Research and development	40	2
Interest	80	4
	661	33
Profit before tax	163	8
Taxation	39	2
Profit after tax	124	6
Dividends	60	3
Profit retained in the business	64	3

Specimen capital employed statement		(000)
Capital employed:		
Fixed assets at written-down value		800
Current assets		
Trade debtors	400	
Sundry debtors and prepayments	80	
Stock and work-in-progress	280	
Current liabilities		
Trade creditors	(310)	
Accruals and other creditors	(130)	
Net working capital		320
Total capital employed		1,120
Financed by:		
Share capital (800,000 @ 25p)		200
Reserves		340
Total shareholders' funds		540
Loans		350
Acceptance credits		80
Bank overdraft (less cash in hand)		110
Taxation		40
Total		1,120

Notes: 1. The current market value per share is £2.20 each; 2. The number of employees is 55 and the total remuneration amounts to £495,000.

Source
Most of the ratios under discussion will never appear as such on any set of printed statutory accounts. The ratios are not likely to be included in any internal management accounts unless they are very advanced. Many ratios, such as those used by bankers to determine whether to advance finance, will never appear anywhere except in their own private files.

Mainly, they are drawn from investigation into the facts and figures which appear in the published or internal accounts, or in other statistical information or in the financial Press.

Those that are published are sometimes fine-tuned to take account of changing circumstances through the year, or from year to year. This may for example be the result of share issues during a period when any ratio would be distorted if the year-end figure were used. They would therefore be averaged by acceptable methods contained in published accounting standards. A change in the taxation system may be another such case. If you have difficulty in reading ratios and similar measurements then you should consider this and if necessary take the advice of your accountant or stockbroker.

It is a question of knowing where to look, but you will soon become practised in this if you are at all convinced of its value.

Shareholder returns and risk
Dividend per share and yield. Reading from the notes and the accounts on page 81 we see that there are 800,000 shares in issue for which the dividend received amounts to £60,000 or 7.5p each. The holders of the shares will be more or less pleased with this depending upon what was paid for the shares in the first instance, their capital growth (rise in their current market value) and the relative risk.

The nominal value at the time of issue was 25p per share (800,000 × 25p = the total balance sheet value of £200,000). This is of historic interest only. If we assume that a shareholder bought his shares for 90p each then the yield for the year based on a dividend of 7.5p would be 8.3 per cent. (This will be calculated net or gross of taxation.)

The shareholder will be more or less pleased with this return subject to his other investment alternatives, the relative risk and the performance of other companies in the same business sector. Bearing in mind that the current market value of each share is stated to be £2.20, he has also shared in some very useful capital growth. This will have been influenced by the demand for the shares and the way that the market as a whole, including the institutions, regard its future prospects.

For an investor the first criteria are the income yield that is received together with the potential capital growth in the value of the shares at the time of sale. It is to these matters that the investor will look first, and it will be on this criteria that performance will be judged. (Sources: published accounts, financial Press.)

Earnings per share and dividend cover. It is not prudent for a company to pay out all of its earnings by way of dividend. Some has to be held back to finance investment and working capital requirements which will expand with sales growth and also as a result of inflation in the economy. Neither is earnings per share necessarily synonymous with cash flow, as will be explained later.

By holding back a portion of the earnings the general reserves of the company are increased. This also serves to save for a rainy day and can be used to smooth out year-by-year fluctuations in performance.

The prudent long-term shareholder is therefore well advised to see if his company has retained a healthy level of reserves to meet these objectives, and a sole proprietor will have the same concern.

Earnings per share are calculated by dividing the after-tax earnings by the number of shares in issue. If these vary through the year as a result of new issues then a weighted average will be calculated.

In our example the earnings per share are £124,000 divided by 800,000 shares, or 15.5p per share, and the dividend per share was 7.5p. It was therefore 'covered' by earnings by a factor of 2.06. This is derived by dividing the earnings per share (15.5p) by the dividend paid out (7.5p). 'Dividend cover' is a useful means of measuring the prudence of a concern and comparing its practice with other like operations or alternative investment vehicles.

Good as it is to receive a high yield the discerning shareholder will wish to know that his company is adopting a sensible attitude to retaining sufficient reserves in the concern for its future security. (Sources: published accounts, financial Press.)

Price/Earnings ratio. We have calculated the earnings per share to be 15.5p per share and the market value at the moment has been stated as 2.20 for each share. The price/earnings ratio will therefore be:

$$2.20 \div 0.155 = 14.19$$

This tells us (regardless of the dividend paid and the yield obtained) that the company is currently generating profits after tax that will match its market value after some 14 years.

If other shares with the same risk, and in the same category, can cover their valuation by a more efficient ratio this will influence us to invest in that alternative.

The ratio will become distorted if there is a sudden rush in value as a result of a take-over bid. In these circumstances the market price may contain a premium element. If such a bid is seen as a danger they may instead be discounted. Either way those circumstances which are reflected in the price, whether they are to do with bids or the economy at the time, will also reflect in the price/earnings ratio.

They help us to compare alternative investment possibilities commensurate with risk and assist in spotting any unusual element in the share price. They will help you to form an opinion as to value when taken together with your own further analysis and disposition towards the shares. (Sources: Published accounts and Stock Exchange quotations shown in the financial Press.)

Asset cover. Many companies achieve very satisfactory profits and excellent returns on the capital employed in their business. This is particularly good news for those who financed the capital in the first instance, especially if they are still holding some or all of the shares.

High profit performance will be reflected in the value of the shares which will be shown in the financial Press (if they are public and quoted) for the particular stock exchange in whichever country they are located.

Sometimes the reported profits are not matched by an increase of cash or other assets in the business. They may be the result of what has become known as 'creative accounting' when figures have been expressed in the best light possible but not necessarily the most prudent. This can be very artificial and damaging and of a short-lived nature. But in the absence of negative publicity it will help to keep the share price high.

A sound, uninterrupted trend in profits will always hold the price high. It will be even higher if future prospects for the company and the industry in which it operates appear good.

Factors in the economy at large, the level of interest rates, new inventions, wars and disasters are but a few of the other external considerations which affect share values from day to day.

With share prices being so susceptible to internal and external factors a new investor may be encouraged to see that the market value of his share is supported by at least an equivalent value of assets used within the business.

Assets per share relating to shareholders are calculated by dividing the assets shown on the balance sheet net of all external liabilities such as creditors, loans and so on. In effect, they are the assets represented by the shareholders' funds to the exclusion of any other liabilities.

In our example, therefore, the figure will be obtained by dividing the assets represented in the total shareholders' funds by the number of shares in issue. That is to say, the sum of £540,000 divided by the number of shares which is 800,000. The result shows a net asset value of 67.5p per share, which is well short of the current market value per share of £2.20 which we reported for convenience at the foot of the specimen capital employed statement.

In the volatile circumstances of trade anything can go wrong at any time. A sharp uncharacteristic fall in the profits of a company that has little asset backing may lower the market price more seriously than would be the case if it were supported by greater asset coverage. The practical implication here is that an organization with huge assets may be more resilient to a one-off drop in performance and better able to recover. In the last resort it could stop trading and the assets distributed to the shareholders in theory may cover the best part of their market value.

In reality, when a company begins to slide its assets are seldom offloaded to pay back the shareholders until it has slid too far. By then the assets will have been badly eroded by losses.

Furthermore, the value of the assets as stated on the balance sheet as a going concern have little to do with what a third party would pay for them if sold. They may consist of special machinery of no use elsewhere, unfinished and unsaleable stocks or debtors that cannot be collected. It may be these very problems which led to the crash in profits in the first place.

So should shareholders disregard this ratio altogether? The answer is that this measure still fulfils a useful function for the following reasons:

- A strong asset base will help to influence a higher offer on the occasion of a take-over bid, the same being true in rescue situations.
- A weaker asset base can sometimes be an indication that the relatively stronger profits affecting the share price have been the result of imprudent accounting and reporting practices.
- Stronger asset coverage per share can be of value in terminal situations, or where the shareholders themselves assert control over the management.
- In the last resort a shareholder is better advised, all other things being equal, to place his investment in a business that has better asset cover than one that has not.

(Sources: Published accounts, derived from above.)

Cash flow per share. Of all the ratios that are printed for shareholder consumption this one can be the most misleading. Its preparation will depend upon the accounting standard in force in each country at the time, but the ratio is most often prepared by taking the sum of the profit before tax and depreciation and dividing this by the number of shares in issue.

The rationale for this is that profit is the source of generation of cash. Depreciation is added back because it has first been charged against profits but is a non-cash item.

Turning to the example, this would have been calculated by adding back depreciation of £140,000 to after-tax profits of £124,000 (a total of £264,000) and dividing by the 800,000 shares, showing a cash flow per share of 33p per share. In this example you may take comfort in the knowledge that this is well in excess of the 7.5p dividend cash payout.

The cash flow measured by this ratio can only be regarded as the kind of 'potential cash inflow' which a firm is capable of creating.

It has no regard for how much cash is dissipated or lost in bad project investment or swallowed up in working capital requirements. The profit for the measure may contain within it 'creative accounting' benefits which do not rebound on the cash earnings at all.

It is quite possible to show a most satisfactory 'cash flow' by this standard and yet have a bottom line bank balance that has soared dangerously into overdraft at one and the same time. Its major drawback is that it is a measure of potential cash flow only, without any regard to monies spent.

If it has any redeeming features it is indicative of the level of potential cash flow that may be available in future years to undo excessive outgoings in any one year. Beware! – Better relate to the change in bank balances and loans over the year! (Source: Published accounts.)

Banking ratios

We will refer to these again in Chapter 5 when discussing the requirements of bankers in more detail. The ratios shown below are the particular province of banks but that does not mean the banks do not consider other yardsticks in forming their judgement.

Interest cover

When a bank advances finance to industry it will obviously have regard to the level of security attaching to the capital. It will make its profit on the margin it charges on its own cost of money thus making up the total interest rate charged to the customer. It is in this sense a commodity like any other.

Nothing will concern a bank more than the customer's inability to earn sufficient profits from which the interest charge will be met. If a customer has to defer this payment it will be added to the capital sum outstanding and the interest charge can then compound dangerously out of reach of the client.

The measure of the ability of the customer to pay is assessed by adding back to profit any interest already charged, and by dividing the result by the actual or potential interest cost.

In our case we would add back £80,000 to the profits before tax of £163,000 to show profits before interest charges at £243,000.

The £80,000 interest charged will be divided into this sum showing an interest cover of 3.03 times.

It may be that the same customer wishes to take on further facilities which will cost another £100,000. This would reduce the interest cover, based on the same year's profits, to 1.35 times. The bank would want to know by how much future potential profits would be increased before contemplating the advance. (Source: Derived from published accounts.)

Leverage

This ratio will never appear on any set of accounts, internal or external, and will seldom leave the privacy of the bank files.

It is quite possible to calculate the yardstick yourselves and it is generally a good discipline to be armed with the same information that is used in the banking community if you are conducting negotiations. Beyond that it must be said that its practical use to you will be very limited.

It is a measure of all of the liabilities of the business (gross liabilities without reduction of any assets) expressed as a percentage of the shareholders' funds which have been committed.

Turning to our example this would be:

Trade creditors	310
Accruals and other creditors	130
Shareholders	540
Loans	350
Acceptance credits	80
Overdraft	110
Taxation	40
	1,560

Total divided by shareholders' funds

$$1,560 \div 540 \times 100 = \text{leverage of 288 per cent}$$

By the use of this standard banks are able to tell what proportion *all* liabilities bear to the shareholders' resources in the concern. Assets are left out of the equation for this reason, and because they usually have little value if a firm is broken up.

Like all ratios, it is one that the banks can use to compare with other organizations. The regard that they will have for any given level of leverage will depend upon their exposure and their experience. Bank expectations are discussed further in Chapter 5.

Break-up value

A bank will consider its exposure to company failure by its past and prospective performance, and also to the level of security pledged.

Part of the security may take the form of a specific or a general floating charge on some or all of the assets. In the absence of such a legal charge the bank must stand as a general creditor if things go wrong.

When assets are employed in a going concern they have a further intrinsic value, or goodwill, as profit earners. When trade ceases this goodwill will disappear unless a potential purchaser is still prepared to pay something for it, and the assets themselves may be next to worthless. The bank will then be looking to the value of the assets on a forced sale basis.

Purchasers will be looking for bargains, the debtors may not all be realizable, the stock only saleable at knock-down prices and the costs of realization have to be faced.

The bank will consider all these matters when trying to assess a total theoretical value on any future break-up. This will be taken into account in assessing the total security for the advance along with any personal security it may require such as the title to the house or other assets of the proprietors.

This is not a ratio but an assessment based on absolute values. It will not appear anywhere for public consumption. (Source: None except through discussion with the bankers.)

Asset turnover ratios

Fixed assets to sales

Our specimen accounts show a fixed asset to sales ratio of:

$$2007 \text{ (sales)} \div 800 \text{ (fixed assets)} = 2.5$$

The ratio is used to measure how many times the fixed assets are 'turned over' in terms of sales value. In our case the fixed assets have been deployed to create sales income at a rate of $2\frac{1}{2}$ times their own value. If everything is in order it will be the sales that generate profits – the higher the sales the higher the profits.

Therefore a high fixed assets to sales ratio is a good indication of high returns on capital employed (actual or prospective).

The special relevance of looking at the fixed assets is that they will normally represent the particular area of 'risk capital'. They will usually be invested permanently with little chance of freeing the monies locked in, so that failure to obtain good returns on them could mean the investment is lost. This is not quite the case with working capital because it is often possible, in the last resort, to stop trading and liquidate it. You may be able to convert all your materials and work in progress into saleable stocks, collect all the debtors and pay off the creditors. The fixed assets, on the other hand, may only be of scrap value.

Nevertheless, investors usually have regard to the ratio of sales or profits to total assets because it is the total that their money is financing.

The ratio of sales to fixed assets therefore is little used in practice, relevant as it may be as an indicator of good health. (Source: By extraction from published or internal accounts.)

Total assets to sales (total asset utilization)
As mentioned above this is an indicator of the efficiency of use of the total capital in the business in producing sales which will in turn hopefully create profits.

A high ratio will also mean that the interest burden on the finance used will be proportionately lower relative to sales, a further important advantage.

In our example the ratio will be calculated by dividing:

2007 (sales) by the sum of:

Fixed assets	800
Current assets	
Trade debtors	400
Sundry debtors and prepayments	80
Stocks and work in progress	280
	1,560

This gives a ratio of $2007 \div 1560 = 1.28$

Many profitable companies have an asset utilization ratio of between 1.0 and 2.0. It is difficult to generalize and the best way of judging this is to look at a range of other successful companies in your industry.

Exercise
Work out the potential gain by improving your ratio.

Show your sales here   _____
Now list your total assets
   Fixed assets
   Trade debtors
   Sundry debtors
   Stocks
   Any other   _____
    _____

Divide your sales by the assets to calculate your ratio.   _____
Now state your target ratio   _____
(This may be the average for the industry, the best performance or your own target.)

Calculate the potential sales based on your target ratio.
(Assets × target ratio/actual ratio)

     (   ) × (   ) ÷ (   ) =   _____

Additional sales which could be earned

   Target sales
   less current sales   _____
What additional profit would result   ???

If you work through your actual and target ratios in the manner shown above you will get a feel for what the business should be capable of achieving at accepted norms for your industry.

You will have seen by your own workings that the total asset to sales ratio has two further drawbacks:

● It has no regard for current liabilities even though they always help to finance the current assets
● The ratio concentrates on sales volumes which may be more or less profitable according to circumstance.

If a poor ratio is the result of relatively high fixed assets, debtors or stocks or whatever, it is more relevant and meaningful to address these individually. This ratio is therefore not one that most people turn to first. (Source: By extraction from published or internal accounts.)

Debtors and debtor days

We now look specifically at one of the most important areas of balance sheet efficiency. Failure to collect debts is the most common cause of liquidations and bankruptcies, next only to substantial trading losses.

Standards vary with credit terms given in the industry, and between home and export markets. At home a reasonable standard for companies trading on net monthly account would be about 60 calendar days' worth of debtors outstanding at any time. Some will get as low as 40 days and it would be most gratifying and unusual to do better.

Debtor days are calculated by adding together the sales of the most recent months or fractions of months until the total matches the debtor value. The days each month or fraction of a month consists of are then added together to arrive at the appropriate total debtor days. Sales are always stated net of any turnover tax such as value added tax, whereas debtors are always inclusive. Before making the calculation, therefore, it is first necessary to take a net debtor figure by scaling it down to exclude the tax.

Annual accounts do not show month by month sales and sometimes the debtor figure is not broken down to show trade and other debts. Furthermore, we do not have a split between export and home debtors, and these sales would almost certainly have been made on different credit terms.

We can draw the information from our internal records, of course. In the absence of this the best we can do is take a short cut which assumes that the sales have been made evenly throughout the year. If we do this then our monthly average sales would be:

2007 (annual sales) ÷ 12 = 167
Our trade debtor total is 400
This represents 400 ÷ 167 × 30 = 72 days

It is far more accurate to make the calculation on a chronological month by month basis, and indeed use it as a very valuable monthly control of performance.

The poor level of 72 days here may be the result of the export mix in the total sales and would be investigated further. (Source: Internal records or use of the above short cut from published accounts.)

Creditors and creditor days

The calculation for creditors is similar to that used for trade debtors. It is the more difficult to match the creditors with the purchase figure. Whereas sales appear in one place in the accounts and usually as one figure, purchases will be allocated to many areas of direct cost and overhead. It requires greater effort therefore to ensure that you are comparing like with like.

It is a useful form of finance if you are that much sharper at collecting your debts than paying your own creditors. For this reason a slightly higher target of creditor days may be your aim. If, for example, your trade creditors equal your stocks and work in progress, you will have the satisfaction of knowing that you are left only financing your fixed assets and debtors.

You may benefit greatly by ensuring that creditors are paid very promptly. This may come in the form of settlement discounts, continuity of supplies or simply your reputation as an honest dealer. It is very much a matter of your policy. If you have a policy it will be necessary to ensure that it is being carried out by your staff because those that pay suppliers are working in a particular pressure area. They will require your recognition of this as well as a full brief.

It must be said, finally, that a huge mountain of outstanding creditor obligations is normally taken to be an indication of serious health problems and unacceptable risk. Perhaps it is time to re-finance? (Source: Internal records.)

Stock turnover

For some reason debtors and creditors are normally measured in outstanding days while stocks and work in progress are reported in months.

Apart from this the calculation is again similar to debtors. Whereas the debtor days figure is worked chronologically backwards into preceding months of sale, the stocks are worked out on forward accounting periods. This is because they have to be of an appropriate level to support *future* sales. If you base the calculation on historic levels of business the result may be grossly inaccurate.

So far as standards are concerned you will want to turn your stocks over at least four times a year, that is to say you will not want to see a holding of more than three months. It is difficult in manufacturing industry to get much below two months. This is largely to do with the economies of production of batch sizes and the mix of slow as well as fast-moving stocks that have to be held in readiness. There is also the waiting time for material deliveries to be taken into account, and non-manufacturers have the same problem with regard to finished goods.

You will not want to accomplish an excellent ratio at the cost of running out of supplies or goods on your shelves. It is therefore very much a matter of balance for each business to ensure that it remains healthy in this respect without taking undue risks.

It is a valuable exercise to write your target stock levels and values on your stock sheets for each item, or rather better to hold this information on your computer. Then compare the actual and target values line by line and see how much money is locked up beyond your intentions, and where. (Source: Internal records and forward plans.)

Profitablility

Contribution or gross margin

There is often confusion regarding the terminology used to describe margins. Contribution is the result of deducting the sum of all the direct variable costs from total sales. These costs will include factors such as materials, direct labour, production variables, royalties and commissions paid directly on sales. The gross profit calculation goes a little further and is after deducting fixed factory or works overheads from the contribution already explained. It is only after we deduct all the other costs of the organization that we arrive at the bottom line net profit. There is sufficient confusion that the reader may well find further alternative or conflicting descriptions elsewhere. To add to this the financial institutions talk about margins sometimes when they are addressing bottom line net profits. For our purpose we will refer to the measure of contribution as described above.

In our example the percentage contribution is shown in the margin of the specimen profit statement as 41 per cent. In a healthy business it should not be allowed to fall much lower. Remember, it has to pay for the fixed works overheads and all the others and still leave an acceptable level of net profit after tax. It will vary with the type of business and a lower contribution is often taken when large volumes are moved in compensation.

This can be a dangerous practice because the business can end up moving massive sales with all the attendant risks for a low return in absolute terms. One puff of inflation can knock out large volume, and thin contribution earners stone cold dead without retribution.

Whenever a company finds itself in trouble and outside help is invited in, the first item that will be reviewed will always be the rate of contribution. Once it has bolted it is often gone forever. It may be the result of high direct costs that have been inflicted through material suppliers, labour pay disputes, performance, or it may be the result of a price war or over-capacity and competition within the industry. These matters creep in over a long time and not without resistance. They will not go away in time to save the operation if they have reached this degree of seriousness.

In view of the foregoing, the rate of contribution may be considered the most single important standard of the measure of health of any operation. If you consider this a bold assertion think about it a little longer. Provided this first fundamental is met, anything else that might be wrong can usually be put right. (Source: Internal accounts and by enquiry.)

Fixed overhead proportion

In our example the total fixed overheads amounted to 29 per cent. (See percentages in the margin of the specimen profit statement.) The financing cost of interest is another matter related to the funding method chosen and is therefore omitted from the calculation.

It is only the reasonable level of contribution that enables the firm to carry this level of overhead and still show a bottom line return of 8 per cent.

It is again difficult to generalize in this area and you should match your performance with others in your industry and in industry at large. However, it is sound advice that you should start showing concern once it exceeds 20 per cent. On the other hand, you will be fortunate if you are able to bring costs much below a desirable 15 per cent.

Before making the calculation, first ensure that the style and preparation of the accounts you are reviewing do indeed properly classify costs between fixed and variable. They are often prepared with other priorities of presentation in mind and you will then have to reorganize them completely before you can make the value judgement. Your accountant will understand what is required. (Source: Internal accounts.)

Profit percentage on sales
We now get to the much discussed 'bottom line' of all our endeavours. In absolute terms a net profit performance of 10 per cent may be regarded as healthy, but remember that it is not beyond the ravages of cost inflation to knock this out in a single year! For this reason some major consortiums will rap the knuckles of their managers if they fail to achieve a relatively safe 15 per cent.

You do not have to stop there. There is no reason why you should not make much more unless you are prevented from doing so in the public interest. Remember the sky is the limit!

There is one major reservation to make here. We have been discussing the return in absolute terms but it will only have true relevance if the net profit proves to be a good return on the monies invested in the business. The converse is also true so that even the smallest profit level can be more than acceptable if the investment made to create it was very modest.

The ratio is well known and used as a means of measuring what profit may be anticipated from any given level of sales activity, but remember the above reservation. (Source: Published and internal accounts and reports.)

Profit growth, organic and purchased
The financial institutions, investors and bankers alike will place great store on the historic trend of profit growth. They will draw comfort from a steady ever-increasing profit record and for this reason many companies attempt to smooth out profit fluctuations

by putting something away in good years to come to the rescue in those that are poor. Despite the need under the accounting standards to show a 'true and fair' view, the practice of accounting is still basically an art, and not a science. There is therefore ample scope to juggle.

The temptation is obvious. All the pressures in the City are for steady controlled growth with as little shock or surprise as possible. Imagine reporting a sudden windfall bumper profit genuinely earned in one year, and then falling from your esteemed position by failing to match the result in the next.

It is valid to use the profit growth ratio but wise, if you are able, to read the unusual features in each year and draw your own conclusions.

What is most surprising is the extent to which many institutions, analysts and the financial Press make much of a successful profit trend without regard to whether it is of an organic nature or purchased by acquisition!

This brings us back to viewing profits again in relative terms rather than absolute. If a consortium shows a respectable improvement in profits, but has had to lay out many millions to acquire it, its performance may be seen in a different light. What you are likely to read is that a company has expanded its profits again by some attractive proportion, whereas its underlying original profit base could in fact have slumped badly.

Some companies, mindful of this, indulge in acquisitions as a means of satisfying the pressures of the City and its shareholders. Once on this treadmill it is very difficult to get off. Remember that reports of absolute profit performance are not necessarily an indication of good health. Look behind the headlines and the figures. You do not have to be a major public company to learn from this. (Source: Public statements and press reports and accounts.)

Return on capital employed

Already discussed on page 14, it is the real acid test and the ultimate result of all our actions and endeavours. It is the percentage measure of profits earned within the business relative to the capital employed.

This capital may have come from you as the original proprietor, from subsequent shareholders, banks or other financial institutions. Part of the capital employed will be financed on an ongoing basis by the creditors as already discussed.

The measure has a very wide and general application to the business as a whole. It has relevance to all those who have financed it or are proposing to do so.

As a general measure of efficiency and well-being it is second to none. If it has a drawback, it is that it is not altogether personal to each interested party. It is not, for example, as direct as the measure of dividends received by shareholders who can at once compare them with alternatives. It is an aggregate measure of efficiency. The capital employed cannot be spooned out to all those with a part interest. It is widely used and the most exacting of the general measures of efficiency that can be applied to a business and used for comparison purposes.

The measure has nothing to do with the method used to fund the operation, and it is consistent with this principle to calculate the return on profits before charging any interest.

The capital employed figure will usually be an average over the period in question. In our example we only have a snapshot view of the balance sheet at one particular date, but we will assume for the sake of the illustration that this has been largely consistent throughout the year.

The return is usually measured gross before taxation. Any differences of a purely tax nature are then considered in isolation.

The return in our case therefore is:

Net profit before tax	163
Add back – interest	80
	243
Capital employed	1,120

This is the total of the fixed assets and the working capital which is extracted directly from the specimen capital employed statement. Sometimes the bank overdraft is included within current liabilities, but this would understate the capital employed because it is part of the overall finance of the business. For this reason it is shown as such within the 'financed by' part of the balance sheet rather than as a current liability, even though it will be on short notice recall.

The return can now be calculated by expressing the profit before interest and tax as a percentage of the capital employed as shown. This is:

$$243 \text{ (adjusted profit)} \div 1{,}120 \text{ (capital employed)} \times 100$$
$$= 21.7 \text{ per cent}$$

Remember, it is a measure of the returns being earned within the business and whether they are distributed or absorbed within the operation. A minimum target commonly used would be 25 per cent. If you start off by looking at the relatively low risk returns that can be earned in building society or bank deposits, and then consider slightly more sophisticated investments such as gilts and bonds, you will build up a profile of possible returns on an ascending scale.

The best of these will be relatively less risky than a business investment. It follows that you will not be induced into business for financial motives unless your prospective return is a few points higher. It is by this means that the standard of 25 per cent has been derived over the years. It is subject to change as returns in the money market fluctuate.

The capital employed total will be made up of many individual projects and product areas. The return will only be as good as the sum of the parts and discerning managers will use great care in making further additions. This is considered in a little more detail in Chapter 3.

Suffice to say at this point that a return considerably higher than 25 per cent will be required on further risk-bearing investments. This will be essential in order to carry those projects that fail and still end up with a diluted overall return of the order required. (Source: By interpretation of published and internal accounts.)

Commercial

Market share

All astute business people will want to know who are the main players in the market. They will obtain statistics of sales from various sources, industry reports and such like, to ascertain what share they have.

This information is used offensively and defensively, and is the basis for market activities and judgement in many areas, including pricing policies.

Perhaps the greatest relevance has to do with the introduction of new products and their likely reception compared with the opposition. Most, but not all, firms have a strong desire to be a market leader or gain total monopoly power. Once you have this you may for the moment at least have achieved a position of relative safety. You may wish to exploit this with much better prices, having first endured losses while seeing off your adversaries. Acquisitions may be involved and you will not know in which direction to turn if you do not have relevant information of market share.

Finally, it is the yardstick by which you can measure your relative progress. It is the one that will inspire confidence in all your staff in a competitive world.

Who can say what level of share is healthy for a business? You may earn a very good living lying low and not becoming over-ambitious. You may feel safer being a major player. If you are you may be able to look to the other main competitors to work together in areas of mutual interest, even though you are in competition. (Source: Published industry figures or those collected privately.)

Home sales to export
It is a sign of greater potential and competitiveness if you have a reasonable level of exports. It is also an indication that your risks are better spread than they would be if all sales were in the home market.

Anything above 10 per cent would be seen as a strong foothold but there are in fact many which are very much higher.

Export markets contain their own risks, not least of which is the bad debt risk introduced by non-commercial matters. The risk to the business is a matter of judgement in each case. (Source: Internal records. Published accounts will give some but not all of the information.)

Sales or profit per employee

The level of sales per employee can be a useful statistic. In the first instance it will depend upon how labour intensive your business is. It will also depend upon how successful you have been in the efficient mechanization of operations previously carried out manually. It is bound to vary according to the characteristics of the particular industry.

Having said that, it is meaningful to research sales per employee within your industry or those of a similar nature. Those experienced in doing so do have an instinctive feel for the level that might be expected. If you fall far outside certain parameters it will be apparent. As such it is a useful quick indicator of obvious over-manning or under-performance.

Since manning costs are usually the most expensive of all, this quick indicator can be used to focus on the general problem. Thereafter it is necessary to get down to much more detail as to the reasons and necessary cures.

The profit per employee ratio is usually too vague to be of any real value. If you can draw useful information from the sales per employee ratio the answers are probably facing you already. The profit per employee ratio is not likely to add much more to your knowledge.

This is not always necessarily so, and some organizations use it as a base for profit sharing. Those participating often bring their own pressure for improvements in profit performance. (Source: Extracted from published and internal accounts.)

Average remuneration

This is one of the statutory disclosures that will appear in the published accounts. It may serve as a guide to the business philosophy on pay and the level of skills that it employs, or simply indicate that the business operates in a high or low pay area.

If the rates paid are several times higher than those of an alternative country of operation this might serve as a reason to transfer production overseas.

Within the home country it may indicate that you prefer fewer, better quality, highly paid personnel, or it may suggest that you have been skilful in wage negotiations and kept rates low. It may be to do with the level of mechanization or the mix in required skills. In each case you have to relate the known facts to the published figures before taking a view.

In our example the note to the accounts stated that 55 persons were employed sharing total remuneration of £495,000. This gives an average of £9,000 per person across the range of skills and responsibilities, and does not have a lot of meaning until comparisons are made. (Source: Published accounts.)

Liquidity

Quick ratio

This measures the ability to settle current liabilities within an acceptable time out of the proceeds of current assets which can be converted quickly into cash. The current assets used in the ratio would not include stocks and work-in-progress. The reason for this is that the raw material stocks and work-in-progress have first to be converted into finished stocks which in turn have to be sold, and then paid for before representing a cash source.

In the example we divide current liabilities into relevant current assets as follows:

Relevant current assets	
Trade debtors	400
Sundry debtors and prepayments	80
	480
Current liabilities	
Trade creditors	310
Accruals and other creditors	130
	440

We would divide 480 by 440 to obtain a ratio of 1.09.

This indicates that the business can cope with its liabilities to pay creditors on a slightly better than one for one basis derived from its own debtors. (At least it could do so at the time the balance sheet was drawn up.) It will pay to look back at the record over a longer period to get a better picture.

Once the ratio falls below one to one the excess has to be financed by other means. This might mean taking up our overdraft facilities, disgorging assets, or permitting a gradual rise in creditors. Sooner or later this will result in unavoidable creditor pressure. There is the possibility of converting stocks into debtors more quickly by raising sales (and production in due course) but this conceives of a different trading situation from that in which we find ourselves. The quick ratio is probably the most useful indicator of your liquidity. Nothing is more vital to your health than your ability to pay your creditors. Profits alone will not keep them at bay. It is cash flow that keeps you breathing. (Source: Extracted from internal and published accounts.)

Cash flow

This was discussed under 'Cash flow per share' on page 86–7. It is not a meaningful measure of liquidity when calculated in the manner shown and explained in that section. It is not what most people mean in general conversation when they refer to cash flow, but it is the way that it is frequently shown in published accounts.

It goes to show that it pays to read definitions and adopted accounting standards very carefully before drawing conclusions.

Current ratio

This ratio follows on where the quick ratio left off, but also includes the stocks and work-in-progress in the current assets used in the ratio. It goes further than recognizing the need for the quick liquid assets to cover liabilities. It also has regard for the need for an adequate stream of stocks for conversion, first into debtors and then into cash. Without this there will be no ongoing source available to pay off future creditors.

It is the measure of the relationship between current assets (stocks included) and current liabilities (creditors). You will see at once that a situation where the creditors are the greater figure will not normally be tenable, and this will be reflected to a lesser or greater extent by the ratio.

Its calculation is a straightforward division of the current liabilities into the current assets. In our example this would be calculated as shown overleaf.

The ratio takes the longer-term view that the stocks and debtors will be converted in time to discharge the sums due to creditors. Money locked up for too long in stocks will not accomplish this, and the ratio can to this extent be flawed.

Current assets	
Trade debtors	400
Sundry debtors	80
Stocks	280
	760
Current liabilities	
Trade creditors	310
Accruals and other	130
	440

Ratio – 760 (current assets) ÷ 440 (current liabilities) = 1.73

Much has to do with the proportion of stocks to debtors in the total current assets. Debtors may be regarded as 'near money' since the concern will be much nearer to banking that cash than that locked up in unsold stocks.

Workable ratio standards have been established by experience over the years. Banks and industry alike normally look for a minimum ratio of two times cover over current liabilities (2.0). This is naturally greater than the quick ratio since it has to include stocks in its number. The example falls short of the standard.

The principle that current assets should be the cash source for discharging the current liabilities is of course sound. It is possible (without regard to the ratio as such) to examine the working capital movements on your balance sheet. See for yourself whether or not you are achieving this aim in practice. The more profitable you are the better your chances because your profit premium will come through in the cash generated from debtors. You may, however, be overproducing or subject to other influencing factors.

While the quick ratio is a much sharper measure of the ability to pay creditors, the current ratio has more meaningful, longer-term relevance. Both are important in their own right.

Before concluding this discussion, businesses which take cash over the counter should not despair if they have a low ratio. They will have no debtors in the first place and their ratios are bound to be lower as a result. They are normally in a stronger position because of this characteristic of their business and have to take this into account in the ratios and in their planning. (Source: Extracted from published and internal accounts.)

Gearing

This is the phrase used to identify the proportion of external to shareholder funds supporting the business.

The shareholders' funds in the equation should exclude any intangible assets so we are looking at external finance expressed as a percentage of 'net worth'. In our example the shareholders' funds are £540,000 and the external funds are:

	(£000)
Loans	350
Acceptance credits	80
Bank overdraft	110
	540

The ratio will be 540 (shareholders' funds) ÷ 540 (external finance) = 100 per cent. In other words, the external bodies have exactly as much at risk in the business as the shareholders themselves.

The higher the external debt the higher will be the interest charge, and the lower the interest cover already discussed. Moreover, the lenders will have a much greater say in the business as the gearing level grows, particularly if trade circumstances take a turn for the worse or interest rates escalate.

So why do businesses take on high levels of external finance? There are basically two reasons:

1. The shareholders themselves cannot provide them or are unwilling to do so on the stated terms. This may be because underwriters are not prepared to back a public share issue or private shareholders do not have the confidence. There are also Stock Exchange rules and statutory provisions which have to be complied with.
2. The external finance is usually comparatively inexpensive, and it provides the opportunity to 'gear up' the rate of return to the shareholders.

Using the example again let us assume, for simplicity, that there is no tax charge and no tax liability on the balance sheet. We will take a range of gearing starting at zero and building up in stages to a much higher level. The position revealed at these individual borrowing landmarks will tell its own story.

The profit before interest or tax will be adjusted to £243,000 (£163,000 profit + £80,000 interest added back) when there are no borrowings. In the absence of any borrowing we will assume that the whole of the capital employed of £1,100,000 is provided initially by the shareholders.

We will change the original assumption regarding the price of the shares which we used when calculating the gross yield.

There being 800,000 shares in issue we will assume that they fund the capital employed of £1,120,000 in full – in other words their individual worth will be:

$$£1,120,000 \div 800,000 \text{ (shares)} = £1.4 \text{ per share}$$

For the sake of illustration again, we will assume that no sums are held back in reserve and that the profits earned are fully distributed.

The following table shows the result of gradually transferring shareholders' funds into external borrowing:

(£000)	Gearing percentage				
	0	25	40	65	90
Shares (price 90p)	800	600	480	280	80
Shareholder funds	1,120	840	672	392	112
Borrowing	0	280	448	728	1,008
Total	1,120	1,120	1,120	1,120	1,120
Profit	243	243	243	243	243
Interest (15%)	0	42	67	109	151
Profit after interest	243	201	176	134	92
Interest cover	–	5.8	3.6	2.2	1.6
Dividend (per share)	30.4p	33.5p	36.7p	47.8p	115.0p
Yield (%)	33.7	37.2	40.7	53.1	127.8

The yields will not in practice follow this pattern exactly because other factors will influence the share price, one of which will be the company progress, actual and potential. However, this illustrates the principle that shareholders who can rely to a larger extent on external funds can 'gear up' their dividends and yields per unit of investment.

If this can be done successfully the shareholders can build large businesses with funds provided from elsewhere. At the same time they can obtain much larger yields on lower commitments to their operations as illustrated.

This method of cranking up returns will be stopped short by the lenders if they find the interest cover badly eroded, as is the case in the example. They will only be willing to advance such a high level of gearing to the very strongest operations because of the burden on the business itself and their own lending risks.

The gearing landmarks used in the illustration are by way of example only and they could be anything from zero to 100 per cent and over in practice.

It follows from this that a high gearing ratio serves as a brake on further borrowing. This is true in its own right, and because of the effect on interest cover. Only the most profitable concerns can gear at a very high level and yet still retain an attractive level of interest cover. Anything that limits the capacity to borrow in this way is central to your well-being because it will deny you funds when you most need them.

In our example we started with a balance sheet financed entirely by shareholders and showed the position that would arise if external finance could be substituted for that of the shareholders. This served to illustrate the principle that an increased level of external finance can be used to improve the shareholder returns. In practice it is not normal for shareholder funds to be substituted by external funds in the way shown. Once invested they are usually there to stay and the external funds are then added tranche by tranche as circumstances dictate.

The figures worked are therefore purely for the purpose of illustration and the actual progression shown will not normally be encountered in practice. (Source: Internal and published accounts.)

Cash headroom

A healthy organization will have borrowing facilities in place long before it requires them. If there is a hiccup in your trading performance or industry at the time you ask for funds this may provoke a refusal at the most critical time.

These funds will be in excess of your immediate requirements but will not be drawn down at the same time since this would result in surplus cash on hand which at best you would reinvest for a lower return than your interest cost.

You will want to negotiate such facilities without paying any commitment fee to cover non-usage. The trick is to borrow over the top of your requirements, but use them in fair rotation. It pays to do this to give the lender some return on earmarked facilities whether you pay a commitment fee or not.

The cash headroom is the difference between the sums drawn down and used in the business at any time and the total available facilities. The absence of adequate cash headroom is courting disaster. To have none whatever is extremely dangerous unless you are unthinkably cash rich.

As to what represents adequate cash headroom is likened to the proverbial 'how long is a piece of string'. Something in the order of a quarter or a third above that in use may be a rough guide when borrowings are at all substantial. This will serve as a fair buffer for the future needs and contingencies, and will just about be tolerated by the banks.

It is essential to remember that your own gearing level will serve as a brake on the sums you can draw down if it is high, regardless of the facilities you have on standby. As gearing reaches anything over 50 per cent you should be ready to re-finance the business by further shareholder injections, rights issues or other means.

Some companies take the level far higher and the practice varies from country to country. What is seen as very high in one country may be standard practice in another, so you have to take local conditions into account.

If you have overseas subsidiaries you will want to consider the practice at home and abroad. Work out a total financing formula for your group which maximizes any advantages.

Your cash headroom may not be what you think it is! There may be limitations imposed on your capacity to borrow within your Articles, debentures or existing loan covenants. This is discussed in Chapter 5.

Exercise
List all your facilities, those in use and those not, and calculate

your own cash headroom by difference. Total your facilities, deduct the borrowings and the result is your cash headroom.

$$\text{Facilities} - \text{Borrowings} = \text{Cash Headroom}$$

To what extent do you think this will limit your future capacity to borrow? Better take a decision to borrow for future requirements or re-finance.

Leave it until the need is pressing and it is often too late. The mere fact that you have planned your finances is half the battle in obtaining them. (Source: Analysis of internal accounts and records of facilities.)

Ageing of external facilities
The ageing of external facilities is a much neglected area but one which can have a considerable impact upon your business at any time.

Unless you are very fortunate, it is rarely the case you can borrow for very long periods without an obligation to make staged repayments from a relatively early point. Some capital repayments start almost immediately.

If all your facilities are on overdraft only, these will be repayable on demand. Were this to happen immediate liquidation could result. The author has often addressed situations where this was exactly the case, and spread the funds between short, medium and long-term at the first opportunity.

If they are all long term, and scheduled for repayment on the same day, that day may be very miserable when it arrives if you are going through a rough patch.

The same will apply if you have only a single facility. If this is substantial you will want to break it up, possibly with more than one bank, staggering the repayment obligations as you do so.

You should build up a schedule of repayment commitments and incorporate this into your future cash flow plans. This will tell you whether they are well spread and assist your forward corporate planning. Those that are still non-believers in the role of corporate planning will have to enter them in their diaries!

Never arrange repayments to coincide with other major cash obligations or plans. The ageing of external facilities is important and it is entirely in your own hands.

Schedule

Funds or instalments repayable:

On demand
Within year
One to two years
Three to five years
Six to ten years
Over ten years

_____
_____

(Source: Internal records only, or upon enquiry.)

Capacity to borrow and security
We have already discussed the extent to which gearing and interest
cover act as a break on the willingness of lenders to advance funds.
Inadequate security will be another factor. It may help to
summarize your position thus:

Lender	Value	Security	Company/personal
	_____		
Future requirements			Security available
	_____		
	_____		

(Source: Personal and internal records.)

Solvency tests

The ultimate guide?
We have so far discussed a number of standards by which we can
assess the health of a business. The great advantage of these is that
they are numeric and calculated specifically by reference to data
already existing or which can soon be extracted.

If there is a drawback, it is simply the great weight of their
number and knowing to which one to pay the most heed.

The preceding pages have given an indication of which
standards are of greater relevance than others. Those that have
anything to do with liquidity are ranked very high indeed, for even

the most profitable companies will be pulled up sharply if they cannot pay wages.

Suppose you have been diligently through the exercise. You have listed all the available criteria and awarded your business marks out of 10 on each count. How do you assess the overall result? Are you healthy or do you have one foot in the grave? Are you counting time now until the day of doom? How will one bad score influence and affect all the others? If you cannot get a feel for this, have the myriad standards been of use to you individually at all?

It is of course hoped that they have been of sound value and also timely. They should at least have influenced you to take action or particular care in any area of exposed weakness.

If we could devise a simple scale which gave precisely the right number of points to each factor according to its importance – one which could then be amalgamated into a single total score – would this be easier to understand and of use for comparison purposes? Is there any ultimate guide?

Any such guide could never be precise because the overall effect is bound to be different business by business, not to mention outside factors, economic effects and individual judgements.

But you can take a view on those matters that we have highlighted as being of the greatest significance. If we have got this right we would weight them in our score to ensure that the emphasis we have placed on them is properly taken into account.

Professor Altman* was probably the leading expert to tackle this problem with a high degree of success. He built up a formula which did result in a single total score based on the most important aspects of any business as he saw them.

By applying this analysis to businesses which had failed he reached the conclusion that any concern would be doomed to extinction if it failed in consecutive years to reach a certain minimum score by application of his formula.

Altman used historic and current data to obtain an indication of what this might mean for the future. The result was a predictive

---

*Professor Edward I Altman: *Corporate Financial Distress and Bankruptcy*, 2nd edition, John Wiley & Sons Ltd, 1993.

health test. That it could be read through a common denominator gave it its greatest value.

He was able to predict that any score obtained over 3 meant that the company should be quite safe. If the score fell below 1.8 then it would most likely fail within two years. A minimum target score was fixed at 2.7 points.

Do we believe it or was he merely playing with figures without any practical implication? The grounds for taking it seriously result from the further use to which the formula was put. Companies were reviewed by him using the formula and predictions were made of future failures.

The standard of accuracy of this forward warning system was disturbingly accurate! His formula has been developed and refined. While the refined version is not generally available, all the lessons are clearly there to see from the original. Others have carried on the development of the principle and created their own formulae, and there is nothing to stop you from doing the same for yourself.

The original formula

For those who wish to test their score against the original formula it is set out below:

$$Z \text{ score} = 0.012 \times (1) + 0.014 \times (2) + 0.033 \times (3) + 0.006 \times (4) + 0.010 \times (5)$$
(The final answer is expressed as a percentage)

Items in brackets are:
1. Current assets to total gross assets
2. Retained earnings to total gross assets
3. Profit before interest and tax to total gross assets
4. Market capitalization to book value of total debt
5. Sales to total gross assets.
   (Current assets and gross assets were both stated gross of current liabilities.)

The importance attached to each is shown by the weightings contained within the formula against each item.

You will see that profitability, liquidity and the relative proportions of sales, current and total assets play a large part, some weighted more than others.

Outside confidence is introduced through the use of market capitalization (the value of the company on the Stock Exchange by multiplying the number of shares in issue by the current share price, if public, or by valuation if private).

We cannot finish here without attempting to apply this formula to our specimen company example (which, incidentally, is completely fictional). First we have to work out the values that we are going to use in the formula as follows:

Current assets gross of current liabilities		
These are trade debtors	400	
sundry debtors	80	
stocks	280	
		760
Total gross assets		
These are current assets above	760	
fixed assets	800	
		1,560
Retained earnings		
These are read off the balance sheet		340
Profit before interest and tax		
This is profit before tax	163	
add back interest	80	
		243
Market capitalization		
This is 800,000 shares at current market value of £2.20 each. (Not to be confused with the purchase price of 90p used in other examples.)		1,760
Book value of total debt		
This is trade creditors	310	
accruals	130	
loans	350	
acceptance credits	80	
overdraft	110	
taxation	40	1,020
Sales		
These are read off the profit statement		2,007

We now apply these extracted figures to the formula as follows:

Fraction	Ratio	Weight	Result
1. Gross current assets ÷ total gross assets			
760 ÷ 1560	= .4871 ×	.012 =	.0058
2. Retained earnings ÷ total gross assets			
340 ÷ 1560	= .2179 ×	.014 =	.0030
3. Earnings before interest and tax ÷ total gross assets			
243 ÷ 1560	= .1557 ×	.033 =	.0051
4. Market capitalization ÷ book value of total debt (A variation of gearing introducing external values as the company is valued by the market)			
1760 ÷ 1020	= 1.7255 ×	.006 =	.0104
5. Sales ÷ total gross assets			
2007 ÷ 1560	= 1.2865 ×	.010 =	.0129
			.0372
			= 3.7%

The company in the example has reached a score clear of the 'safe' standard of 3 per cent used by Altman and we would therefore draw comfort from this result.

It should be noted that the market capitalization will fluctuate from time to time because of economic circumstances in general rather than because of any specific attributes. This does not ruin its validity altogether and the problem has been recognized by giving this element a fairly low weighting.

We mentioned earlier that most ratios affect others. If we improve one it will have a measurable effect on those others to which it relates.

We know that a high level of borrowing relative to internal funds will lead to trouble if the resultant interest charge is not well covered by profits. It may be irreversible trouble if the compounding interest charges swallow up so much of the potential profits that you end up in the interest trap. This is the kind of consideration that is embodied in the formula and which gives it its relevance. If you study it closely you will see so for yourself.

There is nothing preventing you from devising your own formula embodying matters weighted according to importance as you see them.

How well did you score?

Do not overreact immediately if your score rating is on the low side. A number of such formulas have been devised over the years and they are not in themselves a guarantee of anything.

Instead, try to understand which particular features of your business most influenced the final score. Take a view on whether or not these require a rethink or any particular attention.

Statutory disclosures

Their relevance and use

Any set of published accounts will contain within it information prescribed from time to time by statute. This can tell its own story and is valuable as an aid in understanding and assessing the business.

Sometimes it can be misunderstood in the hands of those who are not fully experienced. The author was a director of a company which, in its full history of over a hundred years, was faced with its first real sign of militant action. A strike was in prospect with union members picketing gates and displaying their grievances on placards. One such placard read,

'Look at the amount the directors spend on depreciation', in disparaging tones, and 'What about the employees?'

Since depreciation is the book value written off assets invested in previous years it had little to do with the matter at all but had stood out as one of the larger figures shown within the statutory disclosures!

Summary

We have studied all the ratios and other yardsticks that are commonly used to measure business health.

When you are practised it is possible to take many of them in with a sweeping glance at the balance sheet, in the same manner that a doctor assesses your health as you walk through his door.

Greater emphasis has been placed on those that assume most importance. When these have all been calculated you will wish to check your performance against some other base or the benefit will be lost. Here are some suggestions:

- Your previous performance (that is, establish a trend)
- Line by line comparison with other businesses by reading their accounts and other information sources
- Use of published inter-firm comparisons
- By contrast with banking standards (Chapter 5).

3

How to Appraise Your Future Prospects

Introduction

In Chapter 2 we made an exhaustive study of the criteria used to evaluate the health of a business, building on the human qualities discussed in Chapter 1.

We looked at the operation as though we had taken a snapshot at a moment in time. We were able to look back and establish trends and many relevant conclusions were possible. These served a valuable purpose but all suffered from the common complaint that they were historic in nature. Even the predictive solvency test was based on past or merely current status information.

The result is that they may give the right warnings but after it is already too late! So what should we do?

In this chapter we will be discussing matters of a dynamic nature. Matters that drive the business forward.

We will also be considering the role of forward planning which has, as its base, all the historic and current information which we have covered thus far.

Once these matters are understood there is nothing to stop us from drawing up accounts and other statistical data reaching forward into the future. We can then apply the same tests but this time to figures that we think will pertain to the future. This will surely overcome the criticism that information arrives too late and is only historic when it does.

Having looked at the snapshot we will now discover exactly what makes the business tick. If we intend to remain firmly in the driving seat this knowledge is essential.

Chapter 3 is concerned with the dynamics of the business and where these are leading it in the future. The direction in which our studies are taking us is *forward*. We now view the business in its own right as a *dynamic entity*.

The business analysis

Break-even and the margin of safety

Few outside a business enterprise will ever be concerned with the break-even level of sales or margin of safety. They will probably have a view on the relative risks of the industry, climate or other environment in which the enterprise operates. Beyond this they will look to the level of profits traditionally earned and a varying number of other yardsticks which we have discussed.

This is partly because of an absence of sufficient detailed information.

A break-even chart can tell you what outcome to expect when sales levels fluctuate. A simple chart will assume that all the direct product costs remain uniformly variable, and that the fixed costs remain so without change throughout a wide range of sales. The same could be applied to service organizations or retailers.

If we refer to the example used in the previous chapter again, the break-even chart could be drawn for a variation in sales from, say, £1,600,000 to £2,400,000.

Since the fixed costs are assumed to be constant between these levels of sales they are represented by the horizontal straight line at the foot of the chart. Sales are next drawn in by matching equal points on each axis from zero through to the maximum anticipated within normal bounds. At each level of sales the variable costs are calculated and added to the fixed costs to provide the points through which the total cost line is drawn. Since these will be proportional to sales it is only necessary to calculate three or four points in order to draw in the line. The result for the sample company can be seen in Figure 3.1. From this can be read the following information (which may be checked numerically for confirmation).

- Break-even sales
- Current sales and profits
- Maximum profits
- The safety margin – before profits disappear

In this case a break-even (no profit, no loss) situation would arise on sales of £1,610,000. Since the current stated sales are £2,007,000, sales may drop by £397,000 or 19.7 per cent before all the profits are eroded. Any further drop in sales would result in losses.

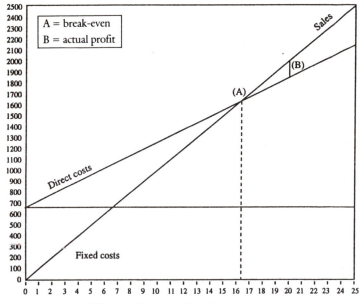

Figure 3.1 *A break-even chart*

It is important for businesses to know their break-even sales levels, and the extent by which they may fall before losses are encountered. They can then take a view on prospects from their forward order book, the state of the industry and so on.

Sometimes they will be working for a single major customer. An example may be, say, a supplier to the motor industry. The industry often publishes predictions of the number of vehicle sales expected in the next few months.

This should at once stir the emotions of the supplier if it falls short of the break-even level. *It is vital information.*

Sometimes it tends to be disregarded because costs do not act uniformly in the prescribed manner of simple break-even charts. But these can be refined and even a rough guide is invaluable.

On occasion they are not used simply because management are determined that they will make any changes in the cost structure if and when the need arises.

This is fair enough but it still does not invalidate the usefulness of the analysis. If more bankers were to ask their clients at what level they would break even there might be some embarrassment among those that have no real idea.

We are now beginning to see the business as a dynamic moving concern that operates within a range of parameters, and not as a moribund, static vehicle represented only by historic performance.

To summarize the study of break-even analysis:

- It is a valuable technique.
- A healthy business is one that stands well clear of its break-even point. Its safety margin is not likely to be eroded in normal circumstances.
- Others interested in the business should be astute enough to make enquiries as to the company's standing in this regard.

(Source: From internal accounts, analysis and hypothesis.)

Capacities

It is not possible to conduct any study of a business unless you know its capacities and its points of limitation.

This information is vital for comparing actual and potential market share. It is equally vital for any kind of break-even analysis. You should know the total capacity within your entire market, or segment of it, if it is at all possible to calculate.

Capacities should then be broken down into greater detail, for example:

- Plant productive capacity in a full year
- Capacity limitation imposed by premises
- Storage limitations
- Export sales capacity
- Individual capacities of those importing your product
- Over-capacity of supply in your industry
- Backlog of unsatisfied order potential.

Such information is vital to all your business and commercial planning. Without it you are much more likely to set yourself aims and targets that are irrelevant or unachievable.

It will be at the root of all your strategies and your business planning, break-even analysis included. It will certainly influence all the figures which you produce with a view to the future.

The business dynamics

In our break-even analysis we used the simple assumption that the fixed costs would not change throughout the range of sales under examination. We further argued that, if we did not agree that they would remain static, we could build into the chart appropriate steps that would indicate the sales levels at which further tranches of fixed overheads would arise.

It may be that production can be contained within a factory up to a given level. One further major order may be the signal that progress will be halted unless the premises are extended. It could be that a sales manager can handle, say, 20 representatives. Beyond this an additional manager might be necessary unless standards are to drop drastically.

These are *trigger points* which you should be aware of and which must be built into break-even analysis and other planning as far as possible. Deciding the points at which these changes may take place is but one of the many factors which form part of the wider study of the dynamics driving a business.

The concept of matters which *drive* a business is important.

The discipline of building up business plans on computer spread sheets (see page 144) dictates that we must know those factors that drive the others.

The level of sales will not necessarily act as the 'driver' for fixed overhead expansion. It is more likely in this case to be productive methods and capacity than sales levels.

The dynamics that drive a business may be internal, ie to do with the composition of the company and the interrelationship of factors within it, or they may be external.

Sales may be directly influenced by the state of the economy, population trends, the number of cars on the road, tourism, those taking holidays overseas, the housing market and many more. The link has to be reasonably direct and reliable before it can be adopted into any serious planning. However, in examining the dynamics that drive a business we are rather more concerned here with the internal behaviour of the business factors at any given level of sales activity. If direct factors driving the sales level can be established this is an added bonus.

Example

Let us now reveal that our fictitious specimen company is engaged in the sale of spectacles through 60 high street shops. It obtains some income from sight testing but the majority through the sales of the products. These are bought from a variety of mass manufacturers and the final surfacing and fitting of the lenses into frames takes place at a centralized factory. What essential elements might we expect to find in such a business which can be described as its driving formula? First, we might find that each high street branch cannot operate without a certain minimum staff. This may include an optician, a technician and three sales staff.

One manager might handle two branches. If they are at all regionalized there might be a regional manager for, say, every 12 shops in five regions.

A region may require central premises for office work and training. The factory may require one surfacing machine for every 1,000 lenses, and these may require 20 square feet of factory floor space. Once there are 10 it may be necessary to employ a chargehand, and for every three chargehands, one foreman.

Every £4,000 sales turnover of spectacles may produce sales of auxiliary products such as cleaning materials valued at £500. If all the lenses were of a simple, similar type they might be priced at, say, £5 each. There may be a proportion of customers' frames refitted or, failing that, a frame may be sold for every two lenses at a given price. The more sub-classifications of this detail the more accurate will it be.

Many of the dynamics attach themselves to numbers of people, production, selling and office space, payroll and sales figures, items of machinery, the rate of production per hour, yields from raw materials and processes, the management hierarchy, transport and packaging capacities, orders converted from advertising outlays, physical limitations and other similar circumstances.

It may be found that the number of spectacles sold varies in each foreign market according to the size of its ageing population. A greater proportion, for example, over the age of 45 will be potential customers for bifocal lenses. This is an established medical fact which will be evident upon an examination of past sales statistics.

These are just a few examples of matters within a business which inter-link and have a common relationship. The example given is purely fictitious and will exclude many of the items that may be found in that industry. Every industry or business is different.

This kind of analysis will winkle out the kind of relationships on which you can place some reliance, given your knowledge of your own enterprise. They will represent the driving dynamics that your business is likely to experience as it expands or contracts according to business fortunes from time to time.

It should be said at once that not every aspect of business is driven in this manner. There are those items that stand in total isolation, are indivisible or purely a matter of policy. These have to be considered separately.

There may be significant differences which you will encounter around any average used for a given purpose. Indeed, this must be expected or you will soon give up on the idea. By choosing criteria which are not far from the mark you will at least know on what basis you are working, and this can be refined by experience.

If you are now asked what will happen to the constituent parts of your business in certain trade circumstances you will be better able to respond by using the 'drivers' you have identified.

You will be using the knowledge to build up your plans and experience of the company like an intricate spider's web, each part coming together to make a cohesive and comprehensive whole.

The total business thermometer

Before returning to the use of dynamics we will look at the business from a different, but very useful, vantage point.

This was devised by the author many years ago and has helped ever since to focus his thinking. It has also been invaluable for instructive purposes.

A total business thermometer for the specimen company may be represented by the diagram in Figure 3.2.

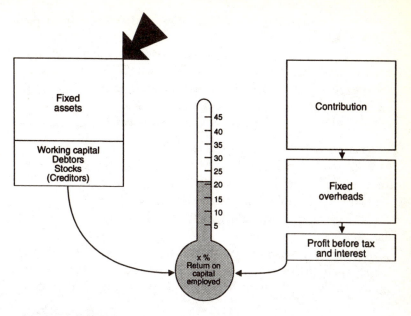

Figure 3.2   *The total business thermometer*

The left-hand side depicts the capital employed in the business represented by its fixed assets and working capital. The right-hand side starts at the top, depicting the total contribution that is generated from all operations. Next, below this, are deducted the fixed costs of the business resulting in the profit at the foot of the page.

The diagram is not to scale. If it were the money value represented by the contribution would be £824,000, the fixed costs excluding interest £581,000 and the profit before tax £163,000 plus interest of £80,000 (equals £243,000). The fixed assets would be £800,000 and the sum of the working capital £320,000, making a total capital employed of £1,120,000. These are the same numbers shown in the specimen profit statement and capital employed summary.

The return on capital employed is depicted by the business thermometer shown in the centre of the page, in this case 21.7 per cent as calculated in the example in Chapter 2.

Note that there is no need to show the part of the balance sheet that deals with the financing of the capital employed. It is the *return* on capital employed that we will want to enrich, regardless of how it is financed.

We stressed in Chapter 2 the importance of a number of separate health checks. Those that are related to liquidity or solvency are critical to the ability to stay in business at all. If given a clean bill of health in these respects then it is the maximization of the return on capital employed which should be our sole financial aim.

The basic ways of improving results

The means of improving the return on capital employed can be categorized in a number of principal methods of attack.

When you are fully conversant with these you will be able to research each methodically until all the opportunities are exhausted.

The following pages reproduce the 'business thermometer' and explain each possibility. The key areas under discussion are emphasized in the diagram by an arrow (or arrows) in each case.

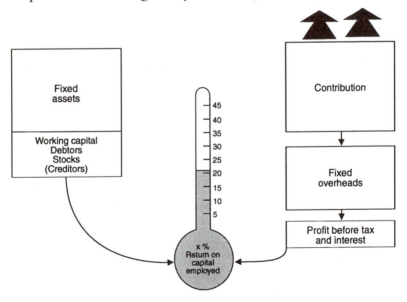

Figure 3.3   *Raising contribution (method 1)*

Raising contribution (method 1) revenue

This is depicted on the diagram (Figure 3.3) by the arrows pointing upwards above the total contribution yield. Imagine increasing the size of the total contribution yield by pushing the dimensions of the box out in this direction. The benefits will flow directly to the bottom line profit and immediately raise the return shown on the business thermometer.

The methods are:

Raising prices
   Straightforward price increase
   Change special deals
   Lower discounts awarded
   Revamp entire pricing structure
   Obtain a relative increase by pruning the product profile or
      service.

Improving the product mix
   Weed out loss-making products (or branches)
   Concentrate efforts on the high margin products and services.

Invoicing
   Ensure that you invoice everything that you complete or deliver
   Check the accuracy.

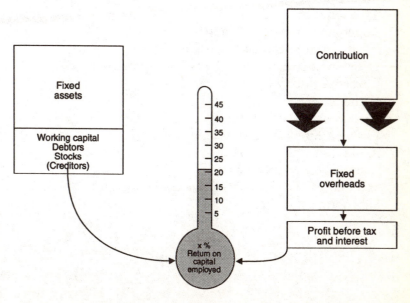

Figure 3.4 *Raising contribution (method 2)*

Raising contribution (method 2) costs

This is depicted by the arrows pointing downwards on the diagram (Figure 3.4). Imagine increasing the size of the total contribution yield by pushing the dimensions of the box out in this direction. The benefits will flow directly to the bottom line profit and immediately raise the return shown on the business thermometer.

The methods are:

Improving productivity
    Better controls
    Enhanced incentives
    Improve training and morale.

Improving yield
    Remove wastage at source
    Introduce quality control
    Use computer-controlled sensing devices
    Use plant performance sensors
    Improve chemical formulae and mixes.

Reducing direct costs
    Substitute cheaper materials
    Apply value analysis techniques
    Improve price negotiating performance
    Use volume bargaining, and pool with others if necessary
    Challenge price increases
    Spend to save
    Update and change methods
    Ensure greater care, adequate instructions
    Avoid throwing away money
    Employ better quality labour
    Manufacture in a low labour cost country or area
    Subcontract if cheaper.

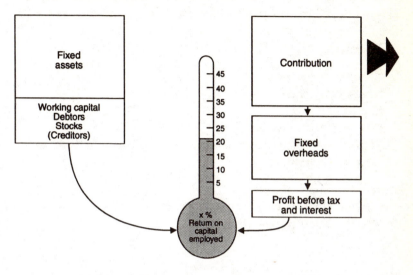

Figure 3.5   *Raising contribution (method 3)*

Raising contribution (method 3) volume
This is depicted by the arrows pointing to the right on the diagram (Figure 3.5). This time we push the contribution in this direction with a similar result.

The methods are:

Increasing volume sales
    Increased marketing activity
    Advertising
    Special offers
    Identify recent sales lost to competitors and follow up
    Raise sales commission
    Appoint selling agents
    Clear order book arrears
    Cold canvass
    Show at exhibition
    Improve feedback regarding service
    Sell by sale or return consignments.

Raising contribution (method 4) new business
This is depicted by the arrows pointing to the left on the diagram (Figure 3.6). We now push the contribution in this direction with the same result.

The methods are:

Entering new markets
  Sell in new areas
  Export
  Widen export activity
  Identify opportunities to team up product with another existing in the market.

Introducing new products
  New products in current markets
  New products to new markets.

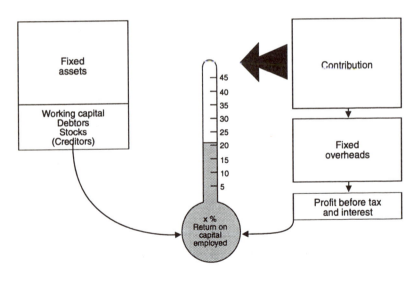

Figure 3.6   *Raising contribution (method 4)*

Reducing fixed costs (method 5)
This is depicted by the arrows which centre on the fixed overheads (Figure 3.7).

This time the reduction of the fixed overheads burden represented in the diagram will raise profits with an immediate enhancement in the capital employed.

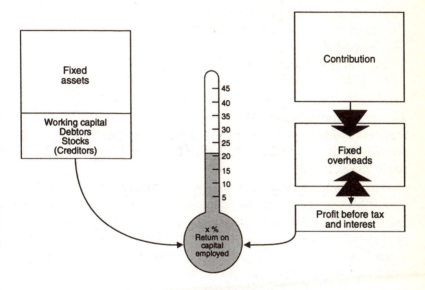

Figure 3.7   *Reducing fixed costs (method 5)*

The methods are:

Occupation costs
   Finding smaller premises
   Subletting
   Changing location
   Clearing obsolete stock, plant and machinery.

Staff and sundry other costs
   Improving the efficiency of systems
   Shedding labour
   Improving general efficiency
   Systematic review of all overheads
   Removal of 'no pain' items
   Avoid money thrown away or carelessly lost
   Improve instructions
   Raise buying performance
   Improve negotiating performance

Use specialists where cheaper
Review legal, accountancy, banking and similar costs and control
staff access.

Research and development
Ensure that effort is being directed to the profitable areas you
intended
Cut out the 'dead wood'.

Fresh investment (method 6)
This is depicted by the arrow pointing at the area in which the
fresh investment will be reflected in the capital employed statement (Figure 3.8).

A company is restricted in its performance by the profit-
creating opportunities and limitations of the projects it has
selected. The return can only be as good as the sum of the parts.

If the individual projects have necessitated the purchase of fixed
assets that cannot be converted to any other use then the above
observation applies with added force.

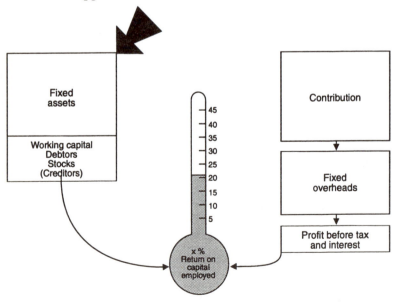

Figure 3.8 *Fresh investment (method 6)*

The methods are:

Fixed assets already committed
Rectify or modernize them
Prune out total failures.

Fresh investment in fixed assets (or projects)
Improve asset (project) selection
(Select those with a return well above the current rate to allow for failures and still enrich the overall return on capital).

Maximize marginal returns
Select those which will already lend themselves to the existing cost and investment superstructure, minimizing total outlay for maximum benefit.

Control the investment cost
Enforce proper pre-investment appraisal disciplines
Insist on submission of alternatives
Deny pet projects that are not sound
Insist on alternative quotes
Closely control the actual expenditure as the project progresses
Subcontract if you only require part of the capacity you are purchasing.

Debtor performance (method 7)
This is depicted by the arrow pointing at the debtors making up part of the working capital (Figure 3.9).

Efficiency in keeping the debtor ratio as low as possible will reduce the level of capital employed in the business. This in turn will maximize the return on capital employed at any given level of profitablility.

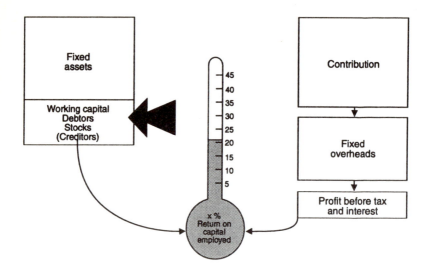

Figure 3.9   *Debtor performance (method 7)*

The methods are:

Use of cash discounts
Withdraw credit and trade for cash only
Contra
Factor debtors profitably
Improve credit control procedures
Vet new customers and review ageing of current debts
Check circulation dates of statements
Settle disputes quickly
Do not send out 'second warnings'
Create your own legal department
Understand the content of any sundry debtors on the balance
   sheet.

Stock performance (method 8)
This is depicted by the arrow pointing at the stock and work in progress figure making up part of the working capital (Figure 3.10).

Efficiency in keeping the stock turnover ratio as low as possible will also reduce the level of capital employed in the business, thereby helping to maximize the return on capital at any given level of profitability. We continue here to concentrate on reducing the absolute amount of capital employed whereas the earlier methods focused more directly on improving profit performance relative to capital.

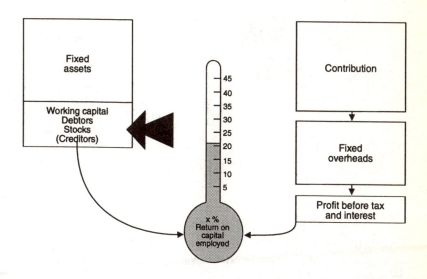

Figure 3.10   *Stock performance (method 8)*

The methods are:

Improvement in stock turnover ratios
  Employ minimum/maximum stock targets for control and
    order replenishment
  Ensure that stocks remain balanced
  Use sound production and purchase scheduling methods
  Avoid stockholding responsibilities
  Hold part manufactured stocks pending receipt of orders.

Creditor efficiency (method 9)
This is depicted by the arrow pointing to the creditor figure within the working capital part of the total capital (Figure 3.11).

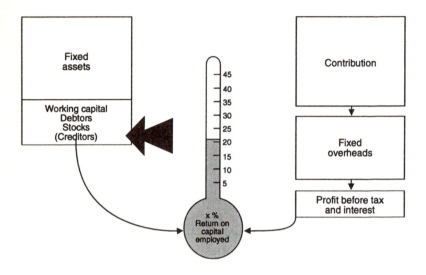

Figure 3.11 *Creditor efficiency (method 9)*

If you are able to defer the payment of creditors then you stand to reduce your capital employed in exactly the same way as with debtors and stocks, to similar effect.

It is not a policy that many companies wish to adopt, and can cause grave hardship, particularly to small enterprises. On the other hand, no business wishes to extend greater generosity to its creditors than it receives from its own debtors. A balance has to be struck.

The methods are:

Creditor payment efficiency
    Ensure that your staff understand and sympathize with your
        requirements
    Extend the staff a lifeline
    Explain how to deal with telephone pressure
    Pay before your supplies are cut off
    Have your excuses or explanations at the ready.

Sale and leaseback (method 10)
This is depicted by the arrows suggesting that the fixed assets are being reduced and the fixed costs of operation increased (Figure 3.12).

In other words, you are about to consider selling any freehold property that you own, following which you will lease it back for an agreed rental or look elsewhere for rented property.

All the elements of this transaction will be executed at one and the same time or you might find that you are at the poor end of a deal or without premises.

This is a slightly more complicated principle to understand but there is plenty of professional advice and property know-how at hand.

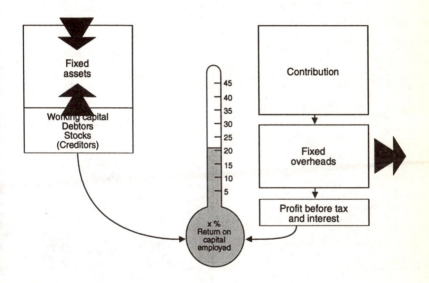

Figure 3.12   *Sale and leaseback (method 10)*

The result is:

The reduction in capital employed

An increase in fixed costs

An enhanced return on capital than that earned prior to the scheme

Failing that, adequate compensation in liquidity or other investment opportunities

Conversion of fixed overheads to variable (method 11)

This is depicted by the arrows suggesting that the fixed overheads are being reduced but the contribution is being decreased as a result of higher converted variable costs (Figure 3.13).

You will first calculate your return on capital employed by inserting the figures of your own business in one of the business thermometer diagrams.

The next stage is to consider the possibilities of converting current 'fixed' overheads into 'variable'. Test this by changing the relevant figures which you have entered in the diagram so that you can have regard to the return before and after the considered action. Some changes affect the capital employed as well as the revenue dimensions, so do not forget to alter these also.

If you like the result then you might proceed with the proposal.

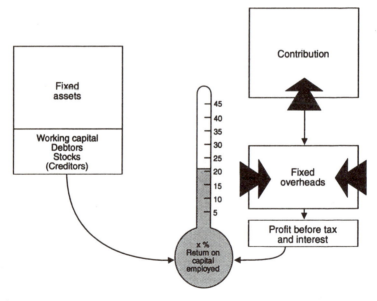

Figure 3.13 *Conversion of fixed overheads to variable (method 11)*

Some possible examples are:

Converting fixed overheads to variable
Representatives' salaries to commission
Payment of labour by piecework or the value of goods produced

Subcontracting work resulting in fixed outlays to the workforce or to outside parties

Reduction of fixed occupation costs by use of variable cost outworkers.

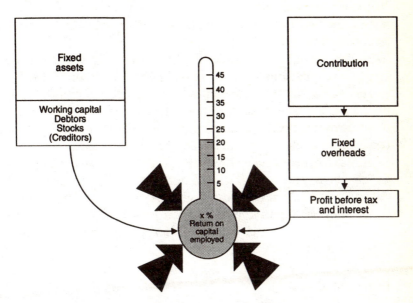

Figure 3.14 *Increasing return on capital employed*

The basic ways of improving return on capital employed
Summary

- Raising prices
- Improving the product mix
- Invoicing
- Improving productivity
- Improving yield
- Reducing direct costs
- Increasing volume sales
- Entering new markets
- Introducing new products
- Reducing occupation costs
- Reducing staff and sundry other costs
- Controlling research and development
- Improving fixed assets already committed

- Fresh investment
- Debtor performance
- Stock turnover
- Creditor efficiency
- Sale and leaseback
- Converting fixed costs to variable.

With success, all these actions will rebound favourably on the return on capital employed result highlighted in Figure 3.14.

There are some 19 major methods open to us, each of which has its own sub-classification for consideration and potential action.

Study these in detail and determine whether their employment could improve the health threshold of your enterprise.

This section concludes the study of the various analytical tools which you may use to obtain an in-depth understanding of the real dynamics of a business. It also highlights main areas for possible action. This leads naturally to the next part which will help us to discover the direction in which our business is actually heading. What more vital information is there than this?

Looking ahead

Inertia and the inertia forecast

We have now reached the conclusion that the review of a 'snapshot' of a business at any one time cannot be relied upon as a conclusive guide to its health; one puff of inflation can knock the enterprise completely off its feet.

We have a fairly accurate idea of our standing in terms of motivation, skills and efficiencies, controls and financial performance criteria. We also now have a better understanding of the dynamics which drive the business and some of the trigger points which we would expect to encounter on the way. But where are we going?

Quite the best way – the author believes the only way – to discover the answer to that question is to plot the path of inertia. This requires looking into the very soul of the business. The exercise has to be carried out with total honesty, without stretching the imagination or covering up at any stage until it is completed.

How is it done? The method is to knit together all the things which we know about the business to build up an *inertia forecast*.

Note that we have not used the expression *plan* because the purpose of the exercise is to see how the die is cast as we now stand. To turn it into some kind of planning exercise would completely blunt the issue and destroy the purpose.

We will knit together the following information:

- Base data
- Extrapolations forward from past trends
- The result of our stated investment policies
- Other stated areas of policy, actions in progress and long-term aims
- Our general unspoken policies and beliefs
- Our views on the economy, interest rates and general activity levels
- Our future forecasts.

These factors will affect every figure in the trading accounts and balance sheets which we will now compile in tabular form for the future.

We will take them forward from out starting base for three to five years, certainly nothing less and nothing more. For the exercise to have full value the author recommends that the figures be taken forward in columnar form for *three years*.

It sometimes takes a little longer before certain inbuilt trends show themselves, but after three years you should be getting some hint of things to come and it becomes less easy to focus too far ahead.

The result of all this will show us how we will measure up by the criteria we have already reviewed, but related to the not so distant future. All the weaponry at our disposal is now employed and we are fully switched on to the forward thinking mode. There is every chance the result may shock and alarm us – even though we may be tempted to outguess the exercise and build in a few exaggerations.

We want to know where we are pointing, using all the knowledge, information and instincts at our disposal, given extra validity by incorporating those policies and paths already set in motion. We will not want to sidestep any unpleasant news by deceiving ourselves at the outset. Nor will we want to violate its purpose by converting the task into the planning exercise. We are now discovering where our fate is leading us in the absence of intervention of any kind. It is as well to know because, if we are not mistaken, this is where we will find ourselves unless we do take action.

The result of the exercise may leave people scrambling in all directions. Firmly expressed beliefs and stated policies may be hurriedly withdrawn. The author has seen stark horror on the faces of executives followed by total denial, even the banning of any such witchcraft from the boardroom! It is often the case that plans well on the way to execution have to be reversed at some cost, or alternatively funding applications may have to be rapidly put in place.

If you get such a result then the value of the exercise will have been confirmed beyond argument.

The result may be delightful. It may on the other hand show grave areas of imbalance or financial difficulty. Do not allow the possibility of doubts or any initial minor embarrassment deter you from your path. This is how we measure the driving force of inertia and benefit from the discipline. It is a more critical medium-term measure of the health of a business than any other we will encounter. Now you have the opportunity to influence matters in an alternative direction – one that will not have been apparent hitherto. To repeat – planning is another subject.

The method
You do not have to be an accountant to understand the concepts we have so far discussed. While managers will leave the preparation of figures to the accountants, most are more than capable of reading them and putting them to use. As the exercise continues you may need a little occasional assistance or you may choose to direct proceedings without taking part in the preparation. If so, you will have to be quite impassionate and detached as we have already seen. An ideal approach is to delegate the preparation to your accountant, first explaining the purpose very clearly. It will then be left to him to collate the base data and glean the requisite views, policies and intentions in each area from the management team. This way you will not be influenced by the exercise as it progresses and the result will be more meaningful.

The exercise first involves the study of the most recent set of accounts available.

You should obtain a certain amount of historic information which we have referred to as *base data*. This might include a plan of any manufacturing facility and major items of plant and machinery, details of warehouse space and product, a schedule of available lines of finance and similar matters which will add to published figures already in front of you. They should all be available somewhere in the organization.

You will be aware of the shape and form of your business and will have to readdress its dynamics and trigger points as the exercise continues.

We will leave it to the accountants for the moment to fill in the background taxation information such as any tax losses carried forward, unused capital allowances and other matters.

We then need a starting base in the form of a balance sheet reflecting the position on a near horizon. This will be drawn up in the manner of that used in our specimen company showing the capital employed distinctly at the top followed by the categories of funding at the foot. (Or the left and right if you prefer.) We do not want to get funding mixed up with the capital employed so that items such as the bank overdraft will not be shown in current liabilities even though they may be regarded as such in statutory terms.

The last published balance sheet will be too historic for use since trading will have been conducted since then for at least a month or so. Striking a balance sheet at the current date is not viable because of the delay in relevant information being entered in the books and for the completion of the exercise.

The method of producing this forward balance sheet is to take the last set of accounts available. Then, using your knowledge of the recent past and your best assumptions about the near future, forecast each item in the accounts line by line to the chosen date. Check that the profit or loss for the period is reflected exactly in the balance sheet, and obtain assistance if necessary.

Now we start to build up a picture of the first full trading year starting with the commencement date on the near horizon. We will build up a detailed trading account and end of year balance sheet, and then progress to the next year. The balance sheet at the end of the first year will form the starting position for the next year and so on until we have figures for all three years completed.

Many of the figures are intertwined. For example, you cannot complete the calculation of the depreciation until you know the level of new capital investment. This dictates that you should start off by rolling forward your intended capital investment and fixed asset figures, probably for each year before reverting to the trading accounts. You will have to use a provisional interest charge until the entire balance sheet falls into place when the funding required will suggest an amended sum.

This will be reliant upon the beliefs expressed regarding the rate of interest that will rule in the economy. You will also have to take a view on inflation levels and a number of other such items that are difficult to forecast and which are likely to vary. It is sound practice if these can be built in in a form which permits you to vary the figures once completed. This will enable you to test different hypotheses relating to the external factors in the economy at large.

It will be clear that all the items summarized earlier will find their way into the result. The base data is necessary to get off the ground. Matters such as unused capital allowances or usable tax losses will at once influence the tax charge of the first and subsequent years. This is but one example of the relevance of the base data that is peculiar to your company and no other. You will probably rely on past trends in debtor days and other working capital performance for the equation you use for future years. You will look back at these to help to point you forward.

Capital investment commitments and ideas for the future are likely to be well formulated, and you will discover these upon enquiry. The orders may well have been placed already.

Many other items required for the exercise will also be in progress in one state or another. They all require research and enquiry but will be largely matters of fact.

Then there are the areas where opinion takes over from fact. You will need to consult with each manager and staff in the particular area of responsibility. Many of these opinions will not have been expressed before because they will never have been sought.

Your figures will certainly encompass matters of well-grounded and already stated policy. You will not change these for the purpose of the exercise or you will immediately be wavering off the track. Long-term aims will be included in so far as they are reasonably well committed and reflect resources and activities already commenced. If they constitute vague day-dreams not strictly impinging on the current business they should be disregarded.

Certain figures will require consideration and a specific forecast will be given, more usefully after reference to any other internal or external influencing factors available.

Forecasts given by those traditionally optimistic or pessimistic may be fine-tuned in mutual recognition of this factor. Any such amendment will be well flagged after mutual discussion.

Later on your forecast will be used to measure the effect of variations of view through the discipline known as sensitivity testing. This has application towards forecasting and planning techniques and we will return to it later.

As far as you are able you will produce a set of single statements which reveal the result of inertia in forward years. It is, as we have said, a measure of where you will be if present influences lead you along without intervention.

Having completed the task you will need to assess the result by using the tools we have studied earlier. There is now the obvious task of deciding how best to react to the results of this inertia-led exercise.

Before doing so it will be useful to examine the modern tools available for the completion of such a task. Without these you could very well be going round in circles for a formidable time.

The financial model

A financial model is a tool which contains all the information that you wish to review in a single series of statements. It will contain those formulae upon which it is built, and which will facilitate changes in all the other relevant areas should any one figure or dimension be amended. You will not want to work your way through the whole exercise again if an amendment is made to a single item. It will require data banks containing relevant information as well as the different formulas that make up the finished tool.

Some will attempt to build up financial figures 'on the back of an envelope'. Any complex and sophisticated financial model prepared manually today involves quite unnecessary effort and consumption of time. Financial models are now normally drawn up and maintained with the aid of computers. Our exercise to plot the path of inertia is one such example which is clearly best developed in this manner.

Businesses, economists and whole governments use financial models for planning and other purposes. They are invaluable as a framework within which to think. They can measure sensitivity and the result of amendments with minimum manual effort and are a truly excellent tool. It is as well to remember that they are only as good as they are written.

You, or your staff, will benefit greatly from their use if you are not doing so already. The techniques and methods of building up financial models are not too difficult to understand. It represents one of those areas where you can build up a complete command of the subject step by step. Nothing more than a desk-top computer is needed at a minimal outlay if you value your business.

Sceptics will properly warn you not to become so mesmerized by them that the day-to-day running of the business suffers as a result. Financial modelling is a relatively modern and invaluable technique which you should certainly have in your armoury.

Spreadsheets

The preparation of financial models on computers uses spreadsheets. They will be recognized by brand names such as *Lotus 123*, *Supercalc* and others.

Once you have turned on your computer and used the appropriate menu-led instructions to enter the program, you will be faced with a blank screen divided into columns and rows within which you will build your model. This is known as the *grid*.

You will not want to continually repeat data to which you will constantly refer throughout your formulae. You will key this into the first file which will be saved to serve as a regular reference source.

If you leave any out, or wish to change any particular formula or field, this is a simple matter which does not require you to duplicate all the other work. You will just add to the data records or squeeze in another line or two of formulas in the appropriate sequence. They can always be amended if they contain errors.

There will be certain factors (other than data) which you will wish to store for use in a number of calculations. These will be stored in a single reference place coded within the grid. This is particularly useful if you intend to update them to meet current circumstances from time to time, or if you wish to use them for sensitivity testing. A good example may be the rate of interest or inflation which is constantly changing and which may affect more than one formula.

Example

You may start off by calculating your sales forecast or plan period by period. If you are the example firm we looked at earlier which sells sight tests and spectacles then you may build up each period's sales by the following:

● State the number of opticians employed each month
● State within the base data the number of assumed tests to be carried out per optician
● State the sales value of each test
● Show the formula for multiplying the number of opticians by the assumed number of tests to find the total number of tests in each period
● Do the same to show the formula for multiplying the number of tests by the sales value per test to calculate total sight test income.

This may take on the following appearance:

A	B	C	D	E	F
1 Month		1	2	3	4
2		Jan	Feb	Mar	Apr
3					
4					
5 Number of opticians		7	7	10	9
6					
7 Tests per optician					
8 (3 per hour, 30 hours)					
9 (3 × 30 × 52 ÷ 12)	390				
10					
11 Total tests		C5×B9	D5×B9	E5×B9	F5×B9
12					
13 Assumed price per test		11	11	14	14
14					
15 Sight test income		C11×C13	D11×D13	E11×E13	F11×F13

The reference to (B9) would probably be flagged up by a symbol to show it is a constant, say, $B9. This would depend upon the particular program you are using.

The formulae are written just as you see them above. The results will be calculated within the computer facility by use of the grid reference that you have indicated.

The lines so far established would be keyed in as they are shown above, but the answers which would appear would be ready calculated, thus:

line 11 (total tests)	2,730	2,730	3,900	3,510
line 15 (sight test income)	30,030	30,030	54,600	49,140

These can be rounded to the nearest thousand or any other requirement.

When you can do this simple sum on a computer you have taken the first step towards learning the techniques of financial modelling.

When it comes to building up a very complicated model (and the type we are dealing with often is) you will probably need some assistance from your accountants and your computer programmers unless you chose to build up the skills yourself.

The figures produced above may be used again as the model continues to be built. There may be references back to some figure or platform already established, and the whole is built up brick by brick until completed. Notice that we do not start by taking total figures and then subjecting them to sub-analysis. We build up the totals from the detailed information first. This way the integral formulae will work and we will have everything we require. We will also have the record of the detail we have used as the base from which to root out any changes or variations in performance. Without these we are left staring at conglomerate figures with no possible means of explanation.

We will of course be introducing our *drivers* and *trigger points* into the formulas we use. One such driver we have used above is the number of opticians employed, since this is the factor which must determine the number of sight tests we can expect to accomplish in any period.

The same driving factor may be used later to calculate the testing instruments required when we will again refer to the same grid reference in the spreadsheet.

Other figures may appear once without having further influence on any other calculations. The trading statements and the balance sheet will be written up as separate statements, one influencing the other. Since you can only build one line at a time on the basis of the information already compiled there will be times when you have to leave one source to work on another. The practicalities will determine the chronological order in which you tackle the task as you will find for yourself.

The secret is to advance as far as you are able on any one part of the exercise before you save your work and fill in gaps in another direction. Sometimes you will run into circular equations. Interest is always a good example because you first have to calculate the profit and assets in use. The assets will be greater if profits are higher, but the level of the profit first depends upon the interest charged, which is what you want to know in the first instance.

If you cannot find a formula or method to deal with this kind of situation do not fear because the computer industry and financial modellers are familiar with the methods which can be employed.

A common method of overcoming this problem is to build in a provisional method of calculation that permits all the other sums to be completed. You then test the validity of the first calculation by a hypothesis statement and correct it to the extent necessary after completing the 'loop'.

Errors to avoid

Many of the main errors to avoid are suggested in the text above. The following steps will do much to eliminate error:

- Remember to work on one simple stage at a time. Then correct any errors after completing the result manually as you proceed. If you do not your mistakes will be locked into the model and you cannot attribute them to the computer.

- Keep the data you will be using separate from the formula chain that you write. If there are no stage breaks, and the sums go on mixing data and calculations for pages and pages you will neither be able to use your model nor maintain it.

- Leave yourself a trail of notes as you proceed.

- Give each major statement which you produce a clear title. Use subheadings and follow a logical sequence.

- Do not repeat information within individual formulae if it is to be used on more than one occasion, particularly if it is likely to change or be used for sensitivity testing. Commit this to one place in the grid for all purpose reference. (Examples may be the square footage of the building or the rate of inflation.) Otherwise you may not catch each area of the model when you make amendments and the model will be inconsistent.

- Round off figures to the nearest 1000 when possible, and take care with decimal points.

- Keep a separate schedule of the assumptions built into the model, and a note of where they lie so that you will be able to identify the end product and know where to make any necessary changes.

- Take care with 'loop' calculations, particularly the interest charge.

- In the model, build in as many checks as you can in vital areas, and ensure that any difference in the calculated balance sheet is immediately obvious.

- Watch the progression of the figures from the balance sheet from one year to the next.

- While you will build up the necessary detail first, ensure that this is collated in a usable form within the reports that you write for circulation. If the work contains irrelevant detail from the reader's point of view you will have to write a report separately. In doing so you will call on the essential figures only by drawing on the grid references of those that you wish to re-state in correct sequence in the report.

- Ensure that the model can be used for sensitivity testing. If, for example, you have committed the rate of interest to a single grid space, alter it and check the result. If accurate you can now make separate individual assumptions about this factor and read off the absolute result and also the effect of a one point change in the interest market. The other items that you may wish to test for sensitivity by one point steps may be sales, margins, inflation and other internal and external factors that will be apparent to you. Remember, there is never one single absolutely correct answer. It is the use of spreadsheets within a range of assumptions, and the speed with which the amendments are made, that makes them so valuable.

- Finally, run the model several times first changing base data, constant reference points, and formulae to ensure that it stands up correctly to manual checks. You should now have a very valuable tool.

The prognosis

Where are we going?

If we have built the financial model discussed in 'Looking ahead' we will know where inertia is taking us in terms of profitability, liquidity and the other important health checks. We will now know whether we are gravely ill or in the best of health.

We should also have a very good idea of our key strengths and weaknesses in each area. Reflect for a moment on your own special position. What has your business got that others do not have, and what are your strengths and weaknesses? We will shortly be considering how to exploit or cover them. Write them down below or on a separate sheet for further reference. They should now be in much sharper focus:

Special position in the industry ....

Strengths	Weaknesses
(list)	(list)

Every business has its own intrinsic value and its own peculiarities. It will have its particular store of human capital value. It will have its own special value to the proprietors or shareholders. Owners of businesses usually have their own additional perks. These may be freedom to choose the hours worked, business lunches, tax-efficient remuneration packages, pride of ownership, position in society and many more.

The financial valuation will be different for a going concern than a non-trading entity. Once the potential to generate profits through trading has gone the business is unlikely to have much value at all unless it is holding valuable realizable assets.

The future profitability indicated by the inertia forecast will say much. Whether we wish to dispose of the operation or not we will now be bound to consider whether the future position depicted by this exercise is one that we are happy to accept.

If we were able to score well when studying the earlier chapters measuring operational efficiency, and in the 'snapshot' health checks, the probability is that the benefit will have carried forward to the inertia forecast. If not, we may have deficiencies in one or two specific areas that we can speedily correct. Where does the inertia forecast suggest we are heading?

Confirmation or discovery?

Managers never like to give the impression they are wanting in knowledge of their companies. If you are presenting your first inertia forecast to others do not be surprised if they tell you that they knew the result all the time, or if they dismiss it as 'something they would not allow anyway'. Remember, the result comes directly from adding existing company data to their own opinions and policy statements.

Just allow yourself a quiet smile if you suddenly detect an air of urgency in the camp and one or two unexpected announcements or changes. Reflect on the benefit of the exercise for a moment. Can you, hand on heart, say that the result was entirely predicted before the task was approached? It would be something of a surprise if it were in every respect. Did your exercise constitute a fresh look at an established truth or was it a first time approach?

Growth, survival or extinction?

Is the company framework one on which you can confidently build further growth?

On the other hand, will your main occupation now be directed towards repairing areas of damage to ensure your continued survival? If there is any suggestion of this you had better postpone immediate growth plans or they may drag you down.

Are you in fact now facing a war against possible extinction altogether? If you think you are remember that your inertia forecast rolled forward for three years so your timely actions now may recover the position.

Are major problems round the corner?

It could be that you are making good profits at the moment and that you are perfectly liquid, and yet the forecast reveals major problems on the horizon.

Perhaps your plans for fresh capital investment water down your profitability because they do not stand the test. Possibly it is the inability to fund their cost that is causing the future crises. Your product age profile may be deteriorating and the future problems may stem from this, being reflected in decreasing sales expectations.

It could be that your trading pattern is forcing your gearing up to the point where you can safely predict that your bankers will not finance you. If so is this the time to plan a fresh injection of shareholders' funds or a rights issue before the opportunity flashes past? Is the problem the result of a major rent review that you had buried under the carpet? Can it be averted now?

Are economic factors playing havoc? Are you about to be caught by high interest rates on excessive working capital levels? The problem may be to do to with inflation.

Legislative matters may be impinging on future performance. These could come in the inability to pass on inflation through price increases. They may be protective and affect your import or export position or market share. It is now essential that you scan the inertia forecast closely and attribute specific reasons to any future problems that may be on their way.

Is action desirable or essential?

You will know from your study of the health checks whether or not action is simply desirable or a screaming necessity. It is important to form a view on this as soon as possible.

Before doing so go over the parameters that were used in the forecast again. You could have given yourself an unnecessary fright by incorporating some outrageous factor that 'goes over the top'. You may have made a mathematical error or built figures into the exercise that are not balanced or are inconsistent in some way. Never use this final review simply to fudge the result. When it has been completed do not sit there mesmerized – if there are problems it is time for discussion and action. It is also decision time because the discussion must not be prolonged.

Degree of urgency

Try to put a time-scale to the problem. If you are running out of finance when will the first cheque bounce?

If you approach the problem methodically you will achieve the best result. There may be no need to rush headstrong into cures for 'phantom problems'. Remember at this stage that they may be the result of evaluating opinions regarding the future or policies that can still be mended by a change of route.

At this point you may require a strong cup of coffee and perhaps a quiet walk while you and the management team reflect on the position. Each person tackles it differently. If action is required how soon must this be taken?

Before returning to the action theme we will consider some of the most usual reasons for success or failure. If you can identify with any of these it may give you a better clue as to what you should do next.

Reasons for success or failure

Reasons for success or failure are legion, but there are more often than not recurring patterns. We can learn much from a study of them.

How often do we hear of the 'one-man business'? This may literally be the case or we may mean that the business is run by somebody with an overpowering personality who keeps all the cards close to his chest and fails to delegate. If anything happens to him it can well mean the end of the business. Others in the business may have a profound effect on its future health and this is borne out by the growing industry of 'key man' insurance.

The business may have all its 'eggs in one basket'. In the 1960s the BSA motor cycle was unrivalled in the world. The motor cycle company had sister companies in machine tools, bicycles, bedding and a number of other products. All these were sold off leaving the profitable motor cycle company in isolation. More than three-quarters of its sales were won in export markets, a very large part going to the United States.

A strike delayed the showing of its new model one year in the autumn. In the absence of BSA a Japanese company won its first substantial order and within 12 months the writing was on the wall for the British group. There were no other activities to bridge the gap and liquidation soon followed.

Sometimes it is the result of allowing the product range to age. New technology is neither sought nor introduced and the products do not receive so much as a face lift. Others will be waiting in the wings for just such an opportunity. There are many such examples which go to prove that you cannot be complacent for a moment.

The problem that sends a company down may be its failure to observe pricing legislation. If the EC detect that fair competition is being impeded they have the power to stop the concern from trading until the matter is corrected. The author once had the task of persuading that body in informal discussions in Brussels that the UK ophthalmic industry was not restricting fair competition through its selective pricing structure. This had been shown to vary throughout different countries in the Community. The argument ran along the lines that the mass manufacturers of the product were exploiting monopoly strength in different countries where their prices were higher, and that this was being orchestrated through the various subsidiaries trading in those countries.

The truth was that each subsidiary charged whatever the local market would bear. The parent was without knowledge, let alone dictating the tune. Furthermore, the reason for the variations was the need to respond to much fiercer competition from other main players in the world industry, and as a response to price discounting. The differences in prices were not so much a sign of exploitation of power but rather indicative of very fierce forces of competition which needed little assistance from Brussels. The point was accepted and the company heard no more, but another trading in the UK was not so fortunate. Failing to cooperate fully, it received a visit from EC administrators (acting under the Treaty of Rome competition rules) who removed the files and stopped all activity dead. Such perils can fall on any company at any moment.

Other bodies with similar powers are those that investigate shortcomings in the control and use of dangerous chemicals and other industrial substances or manufacturing processes. If they declare a process dangerous they have the power to stop production immediately. It may take the firm concerned months to install safer methods or equipment. Its cost may combine with the lost revenues in the interim period to sink the firm altogether. The reinvestment may simply not be worthwhile for some.

The product may fail to satisfy its customers because of poor quality or design. Once the word gets around there may be no prospect of recovery. Sales will fall so quickly that any cost-cutting response will be too late. The same applies with equal force in the service industry.

A cheaper alternative may knock you out, especially if your product is over-specified for its purpose. Its country of origin may be one in which labour rates are very low or where it is suddenly able to take advantage of a new breakthrough in technology.

The application of a country's taxation system may knock out demand. A change in policy towards items provided free in a country's health care system may deal the final blow.

The business may trade from particular premises that are affected by adjacent development activity. If the street is sealed off to customers you will lose your business very quickly if you cannot react.

Accidents, fires and acts of nature take their considerable toll. Unfortunate rumours can be equally devastating. We will give more examples which are deserving of their own category. Some of these involve shooting yourself in the foot. In these cases the fault may be attributed entirely to the management and to no other factor or person.

Market saturation

It sometimes happens that new competition is drawn to a market as though to a modern-day gold rush.

Individual companies may build up their manufacturing capacities and stocks based on optimistic views of their prospects, or foreign stocks may flood the market on the cessation of trade of an overseas giant.

The total demand in the market may itself be shrinking. It all leads to the same end – too many goods chasing well satisfied customers.

Recession

We all know to our cost that a recession extracts so much spending power from the market that firm after firm goes to the wall. One firm's closure can immediately affect another, perhaps its component supplier or provider of a service. The more that go into liquidation the greater is the number of unemployed people, meaning still less consumer spending and continuing business failures.

Inflationary erosion of profits

Economists argue that a small, gradual amount of inflation is a good thing. They explain that it acts as a lubricant in the economic system, allowing for flexibility and selection by choice. It will finance and generate job mobility and movements towards certain goods and services. It separates the 'men from the boys' so that the healthy survive at the expense of the weak and inefficient, to the ultimate benefit of the nation.

The most efficient will not need to pass on their own inflation in price increases. They will apply value analysis techniques to the product, introduce benefits through productivity and become increasingly efficient in all departments. Some may force costs down by obliging their workers to take negative pay awards.

It is indeed true that those well equipped in these areas will be successful up to a point in just this manner. However, it is not possible year after year to go on relying solely on this means without passing on cost inflation to your customers.

If your business is at all typical, you will have to pass on your cost inflation at least once annually in one form or another. If you do not do so your profits will be totally eroded in next to no time. When your contribution (or gross margin) has gone there may be no second chance.

Inflationary erosion of profits happens in one of four ways:

- As a defence in a price war when costs still rise
- As an aggressive ploy to win market share
- By competition or statutory control
- By neglect.

If you are making 10 per cent profit on sales before tax this might give you a good return on capital employed and generate a healthy cash flow.

Think how quickly a typical inflation rate increase across all your costs could wipe these profits out completely. You cannot afford to let it happen by neglect or through foolish market optimism.

Competition

You compete on more than just price and quality. There is also delivery, after-sales service, innovation and general publicity. The competition can take you out of business on any of these counts.

Management incompetence

This covers a variety of sins. Insufficient time may be spent in the business or it could be totally disorganized and inefficient. None of the virtues discussed in Chapter 1 may be present and poor judgement, in particular, may be the most vital factor.

Every manager makes mistakes and learns from experience. If you are terrified of the consequences of any decision you may never make any. Weigh up the risks behind your decisions and avoid 'lose all' situations.

Lack of planning

If you do not plan ahead you may fall victim to a number of disasters. Quite the worst is that of running out of cash. Your lack of planning will be self-evident to your bankers who will not automatically support you simply because you are profitable.

If your management skills are found wanting and there is no planning discipline they will form the view that your business is totally out of control. Would you put your money in such a business?

No costing

Here again the absence of costing disciplines means that you will never know your real margins. You could be pouring money down the drain until the receiver is eventually called in.

Banking prejudice

Sometimes a whole industry, or a major sector within it, falls victim to circumstance. Business after business in the industry may be reporting trading difficulties brought about by circumstances beyond its control.

If this is the case the banks will be swift to form an opinion and they may well decide to exercise much greater caution or avoid exposure altogether.

You may not be a victim of the trading difficulties. If you are you may feel that you will survive them in time, given support. In either case support may not be forthcoming and you may go under as a result.

Overtrading

Your expansion may have been too quick and too demanding on your cash resources. One of the most common causes of failure is that of overtrading. Your very success could bring you down.

Your sales base will increase rapidly sucking all your cash facilities into manufacture and supporting debtors.

There will not have been sufficient time to experience handling the increased level of activity, and no opportunity to build up adequate reserves in the company.

Production facilities may creak at the seams and the management team be too far stretched. The accounts staff may even have difficulty in keeping abreast of the invoices and raising statements on time.

You may find that you fail to meet your customers' orders. Your failure to manage may lead to increasing stocks and the total lack of funds and organization may lead to pressure from creditors and the withdrawal of supplies.

A sudden reversal of fortunes in these circumstances can be the trigger that brings the whole business down. It could come in the form of bad debt experience, an unexpected cost increase, eroding margins on the increased sales, or from a variety of directions.

The bank manager may be the next person to knock on the door to restrict your growing overdraft. You will need all your tenacity to harness the business and bring it back in line.

Your first line of defence may be a price increase. If it does not cool down the demand it will at least ensure an improved cash intake and raise profits. This may not of course be the final answer.

Dilution of main activity

There are many factors that persuade a company to provide all things to all men. They will not want to see their customers go elsewhere for any goods they can provide in their chosen product area.

Some products can only ever produce profits on a certain scale. If you take these on board without the requisite scale you can very easily dilute your main profitable activity.

The more you take on the more complicated the business becomes in general. It becomes easy in these circumstances to take on more levels of management to deal with the problem until such time that the entire operation is prejudiced.

It is all a question of balance between having too little or too much in your product profile. All your eggs in one basket or dilution of returns at the other extreme!

Interest strangulation

If you have a high borrowing debt and poor interest cover you are in a particularly vulnerable position. This is especially true when there is a sudden sharp increase in the rate of interest.

This may leave you in a position where, profitable or otherwise, you are not generating enough cash to meet the charge. With each month that passes the unpaid interest costs will compound eroding the extent to which they are covered still further.

Businesses in this position find they are fighting an up-hill battle. The point is reached where the level of sales attainable can only result in so much profit, and this will no longer match the compounding interest element whatever action is taken. If the cure is administered too late then interest strangulation is the certain result.

The symptoms

There are tell-tale signs that are not necessarily conclusive evidence, but which can be a good indication of problems ahead.

Some of these are:

- Ageing management
- No executive appointments to the board
- Old-fashioned machinery
- Premises in need of repair or decoration
- Low morale and outmoded attitudes
- Takeover rumours
- Hurried meetings
- Out-of-date marketing
- Delays in responding to trends
- No new products
- Late invoices
- Illness and absenteeism
- Increased legal activity
- Deferred price increases
- Late deliveries
- High returns and debit notes
- Mounting stocks
- Raised voices
- No computer costing or planning
- The use of 'creative accounting'
- Late accounts and a worried-looking finance director
- No finance director.

The self-destruct mode

If you enter the self-destruct mode the symptoms will scream at you.

It occurs usually when avoiding action is left too late. There is a sudden and violent surge of activity, cost cutting and the removal of staff and directors. This results in a reduction in the level of service given to the customer. The cancellation of orders then necessitates further activity on the cost-cutting front to the point where the remaining staff simply do not have the capacity or skills to hold the situation.

Performance and cancellation of business both go into a dive, ever spiralling downwards into eventual oblivion. It is then too late to do anything about it. These symptoms cannot be missed.

Avoiding the pitfalls

The ways of avoiding the pitfalls will largely be self-evident.

You will have to be ever vigilant and conscious of all the matters that can go wrong. Do not allow these to depress you. Rest in the comfort of knowing you have considered them all scientifically and methodically. Your margin of safety should be much enhanced. Any danger can only arise now from the unpredictable or unknown.

Try to make your product the brand leader. Ensure as far as possible that it is unassailable. Spread your management among a well-motivated and well-trained team. Delegate so that everybody is working near the threshold of their abilities. Avoid keeping all your eggs in one basket and do not let your product profile age without notice. Monitor your market share and keep a close eye on the actions of your competitors. Keep abreast of inflation by whatever means possible.

Be methodical. Do not pass over the need to use up-to-date costings and accounts. Use planning techniques and take a look at the future through the inertia forecast. Monitor all the important ratios and other health measures and respond with the appropriate action.

Go looking for trouble and eradicate it before it arrives. In other words, have faith in the value of risk management in all its forms.

4

Action

Action priorities

By now you should have a very good idea of the state of health of your business. Whatever the condition, it is likely that you will now be fully switched into the action mode.

The most profitable businesses are always working to maximize their results, and do not lack inspiration because they are in difficulty. Attempts to improve any given situation will fail if we rush headlong into action without setting some priorities, which will depend upon the particular condition.

It is safe to say, however, that you will want to look at your *cash headroom* first. While others are given the task of improving working capital performance, collecting debts and the like, your attention will turn to the contribution rate.

First check its calculation. If there is a large proportion of direct variable costs accounted for as general overheads you will be thrown completely in the wrong direction.

List all the areas where you contemplate action as they occur to you and then rank them in order of priority for maximum impact on cash flow and profitability.

Identifying the cause of loss-making products should top the list. If you cannot eradicate the cause get rid of the product quickly. Do not forget to include a search for bottlenecks. These are often the root cause of major problems.

If you have started with a detailed search of the representatives' expense sheets you have certainly gone off in the wrong direction.

What approach do we take?

The approach taken will largely depend upon the level of urgency involved.

The following are the main approaches that you may adopt according to the level of urgency. Some of them are taken directly from the basic ways of improving returns on capital employed first shown in Chapter 3 and explained here in greater detail. Others give examples of the different approach routes which you may adopt, and which lead to one or other of the basic methods of improving returns:

- The systems approach
- The natural wastage route
- Progressive reduction
- Volume bargaining
- The value analysis route
- Converting fixed to variable
- Subcontract
- Selectivity
- Efficiency improvements
- Incentives
- Spending to save
- Fine tuning
- Swinging the axe
- Reaction management
- The complete rebuild.

The systems approach

This is a method of cost cutting which involves the scientific simplification of systems in use, following which staff savings can be implemented painlessly and without loss of efficiency. You start off by writing a flow chart of all the actions and paperwork involved at each stage in the total system. The length of this when complete will tell you much. The longer the system specification the more people will it employ. Streamline the procedure and you will benefit with no pain to the business.

We would start by listing all the major systems in operation. They will involve paperwork and people in areas such as the following:

- Ordering goods and services and checking their receipt in good condition
- The procedures for the payment of goods and services
- The delivery, invoicing and debtor collection for goods and services sold
- Stock control and perpetual inventory methods
- Production scheduling
- Submitting quotations.

These are just a few examples and there will be many more.

Commit one system at a time to paper and follow each copy of the docket set in use through the procedure, making careful notes at each stage of what occurs until you get to the end. Interview people at each stage. You will probably find that many don't know where the paperwork came from and what happens to it next – even less will they all understand the consequence of handling errors.

In many instances you will be able to find short cuts. If your staff go through all the same detail to build up estimates for quotation purposes on each occasion you may short-circuit this by using a near standard formula for similar types, and fine-tuning it by exception only.

You may find that the arrival of one docket set triggers the unnecessary raising of another supplementary docket set. Worse, you may find that your (conscientious) staff are steadfastly hanging on to the old system that you replaced years ago in tandem with the new, 'in case the new system goes wrong'. This philosophy will most likely have added even more numbers to your total staff.

You must of course retain all the vital internal checks properly built into the system, but you may have a field day. The problem may be the absence of a suitable system where one is required. Pre-printed paperwork containing adequate instructions does much to simplify and de-skill the job functions, and a printed manual is an extremely useful 'bible'.

The author once prepared a flow chart for an operation within an international rubber group. It contained three docket sets, 80 operations and dozens of staff to get the goods out of the door and paid for. The flow chart was feet long. Its reduction saved man years of work after some redundancies and redistribution of work.

It didn't end there, either. There were space savings, as surplus offices became available. Heating and rental costs were reduced, telephone calls and other labour oncosts. When accomplished the general level of efficiency is improved and the benefits are long lasting.

In another example at the same company the author was involved in an investigation into the rates paid to haulage companies for delivering its tyres to depots. This was thought of by most as a rather humdrum task that was carried out annually to show that it hadn't been overlooked.

Quotations obtained proved that savings could be made, but on-site observation revealed startling facts. A great many of the lorries weaving in and out of the site were carrying production waste off to a tip. The cost of this part of the carriage and tip charges was high, but nothing like the value of the re-usable rubber and offcuts that had fallen off the production track. The group had after all paid very dearly for bringing this expensive material all the way from Malaya.

The work-force was paid by piecework and was responsible for taking the off-cuts, fallen material and chippings to a soulless place where they were fed into lifts and taken to a re-processing plant manned by about six persons and dedicated to recycling the material. The pure rubbish was to be separated and placed at a point further up the bay for collection for tipping by the hauliers.

The area was full of carbon-black dust and few strayed there, except the author on the occasion of the investigation, and the work study team the group had employed to reduce costs. They had recommended the dismissal of the deck supervisor whose only function was to supervise what went where. After all, the production operators could direct the good material towards the lift for recycling, or so they thought. Not likely. They were too busy scampering back to earn their piecework monies and ensure they were in place as the production line was working ever faster.

The hauliers took as many loads as they could without murmur. In fact they took many half loads and expanded their truck fleet on the back of their unsupervised journeys. We were paying for our own highly expensive material to be taken off to the tip at still further cost.

What was the recycling team doing about this you ask? Ignoring the expensive recycling equipment and enjoying a good game of cards. Life was so good one even brought his bed in.

This operations research type of systems review started off with a simple pricing check, but exposed the loss of many millions of pounds within these areas:

- Haulage rates
- Half loads
- Tipping charges
- Wasted raw material
- Idle recycling machinery
- Idle staff.

The natural wastage route

A stop is placed on the replacement of any employees who leave unless sanctioned by the chief executive. The reduction in numbers employed is allowed to continue progressively until the position is restored or the remaining staff cannot take up the strain of the extra work. It has the advantage that it can be absorbed gradually and without redundancies or dismissals.

Progressive reduction

This is similar to the natural wastage route in that it is also comparatively slow and progressive. The difference is that the management do not wait for employees to leave of their own accord but take the lead themselves. The advantage of this is that they can take people out where they most suspect they are over-manned.

Volume bargaining

In its price negotiations with its suppliers, the business takes maximum advantage of any large-scale purchases, whether for services, materials or goods. It may pool with others in the same group or elsewhere in order to equip itself with buying muscle. Major areas of expenditure will be tackled first.

A Health Check for Your Business

The value analysis route

All products and services are thoroughly examined with the aim of finding a cheaper alternative method of providing the service or manufacturing the product. Cheaper materials may be substituted in the manufacture of the product, its appearance or its packaging. The functions may be simplified or bought-in units substituted for made-in parts. It may be completely redesigned. All areas are inspected with the aim of cost reduction without impairing the demand for the item. Profits can be maximized through this route with little or no capital investment. Consider this in contrast to new investment projects which may give no better returns at far higher cost, and take much longer to come on stream.

Converting fixed to variable

All trading operations go through periods when sales income fluctuates. The demand for public sector services, or the monies that can be spent on them, also fluctuates in like manner.

This may result in a reduction of the total margin or contribution. The fixed overheads will be the same at this time and the profit will fall or convert into a loss. The greater the proportion of fixed overheads the more severe the problem – and the lower the margin of safety.

A permanent loss of sales in these circumstances can be devastating. One of the least risky routes therefore is to attempt to convert as many fixed costs as possible into costs of a variable nature. The following example will illustrate the point.

You are running a multi-packaging company. It takes delivery of chocolate bars from the manufacturer and places them into dozen-pack special offer promotional wrappings on behalf of the manufacturer. Many work in this way since the promotions are sporadic and too consuming of their own space and attention.

They also shrink wrap certain products, and pack Christmas cards into boxes of 30 all through the year.

The multi-packaging concern pays about 10 per cent of the sales value for its wrapping materials, and employs one person full time in agreeing the promotional requirements and quality required. His salary is £23,000. Total sales amount to £600,000.

Twenty-one local women are paid £7,700 annually (including oncosts) for the actual wrapping operations, Christmas card sorting and other tasks. They are found to be more dexterous than men. They work in teams and it is difficult for the most part to lose one or two members without disbanding the whole section.

Attached to each team are two indirect workers preparing the materials and feeding the line, and one supervisor. The indirect workers receive £9,000 each, and the supervisors £14,000. This all takes place in a warehouse of 10,000 feet rented on a 21-year lease at an annual sum of £60,000.

There are three sales staff on the road seeking new business and their salaries in each case are £15,000. Other administrative staff are paid a total of £36,000, and the two management partners pay themselves £25,000 each. If you were asked to draw up the profit and loss account of this operation it might look like this:

		£	%
Sales		600,000	100.0
Wrapping materials		60,000	10.0
Direct labour	21×7700	161,700	27.0
		221,700	37.0
Contribution		378,300	63.0
Warehouse rental		60,000	
Indirect labour	2×3×9000	54,000	
Supervision	3×14,000	42,000	
Admin staff		36,000	
Publicity manager		23,000	
Sales staff	3×15,000	45,000	
Management	2×25,000	50,000	
Total fixed overheads		310,000	51.6
Profit		68,300	11.4

You are informed that sales in the future are not likely to exceed £700,000, but that the business formula (the 'dynamics' of the business) are likely to remain the same.

A break-even chart for this business in shown in Figure 4.1.

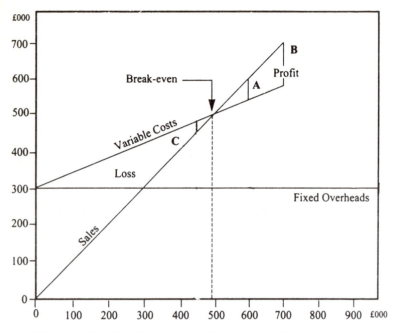

Figure 4.1 *Break-even chart for multi-packaging company*

You will be able to read off the chart the current trading situation and profit of £68,300 on sales of £600,000 at 'A'. If maximum sales of £700,000 are achieved the chart at 'B' shows that the profit will be £131,000 (a creditable 18.7 per cent of sales). Break-even occurs on sales of £492,000 (to the nearest £000). Therefore the sales can drop from the present level of £600,000 to £492,000 before any further fall results in losses.

That is to say the all-important margin of safety is 18 per cent. This is none too good a safety margin – not that surprising considering that fixed overheads account for such a high percentage of sales. (See the profit and loss account.)

The worst then happens. Sales fall to £440,000 due to a turn in fortunes, and no recovery is foreseen for at least a year or two. The level of losses read off the break-even graph at 'C' amounts to £32,800, and the bankers are already expressing grave concern. It is a case of drastic changes now or no jobs for anybody – indeed no company! A meeting of all staff is called to hear the following proposals:

- The three teams, their indirect workers and the supervisors will all have to pull their weight and be rewarded purely on a results basis. This total work-force will in future be paid a percentage of good work invoiced weekly to the customer. This will save the firm paying for lost time and other inefficiencies, and give the labour-force an incentive to work together with greater flexibility. The supervisors will agree the manning levels necessary with the workers, any necessary job-sharing arrangements and similar considerations. They will also be asked to step in to rescue trainees who might slow down the line, and generally play a more active part.

  This will make the labour cost truly variable with sales. The action taken is expected to improve efficiency and output by at least 15 per cent. The percentage to be paid to the work-force is pegged at 40 per cent of the old levels, but after adjustment for the minimum efficiency improvement anticipated.

  There will be no upper limit to the amount which can be earned by the work-force provided it is based on good invoiceable work. Some staff will be pleased to spend a little more time at home with their families, and there will be the opportunity for all to earn considerably more through their own efficiency when sales rise.

- The major customers have agreed that they will be better placed to organize the procurement of the promotional material. This will not only reduce its cost to 7.5 per cent of sales, but also take out the need for the company to employ the publicity manager.

- The remuneration package of the salesmen will be revised. They will each earn £10,000 as basic salary, but be paid a further 2 per cent commission on sales without upper limit.

- The lease agreement contains a break clause enforceable shortly which will free one-third of the space rented. Notice will be given immediately and a more efficient layout will make it possible to work in the reduced area. With minimal expenditure the reduced space can be made to work at much higher future levels of business.

- Finally, the management partners will reduce their salaries immediately by 10 per cent and introduce a results-related bonus for any further earnings as soon as equitable details can be worked out.

There is much debate and some recrimination, but there is little alternative, and the fresh business plans are accepted by all without change. In fact, many of the workers are eager to accept the challenge and fresh opportunities. None of them wishes to lose their job which would be the only alternative.

So where does this leave the company? If the profit and loss account for a full year was now redrawn to reflect the new circumstances is would appear as follows:

Sales		440,000	100.0
Wrapping materials	7.5%	33,000	7.5
Labour	40%×440000÷1.15	153,000	34.8
Sales commission	2%	8,800	2.0
		194,800	44.3
Contribution		245,200	55.7
Warehouse rental		40,000	
Admin staff		36,000	
Salesmen – basic pay		30,000	
Management		45,000	
Total fixed costs		151,000	34.3
Profit		94,200	21.4

Now we have a much improved break-even chart (Figure 4.2).

A handsome profit has been carved out of the operation at the same level of sales that previously gave rise to the crippling losses.

Profits of £94,200 replace losses of £32,800 (A). If the previous level of sales returns profits will now be £238,900 on £700,000 (or 34%) (B). Even a partial recovery will bring much enhanced results.

Break-even point has been lowered to sales of only £271,000 so that the margin of safety is now a much safer 38 per cent. The atmosphere is now much better and the future looks rosy despite the setback. See how far the break-even line has moved to the left of the graph.

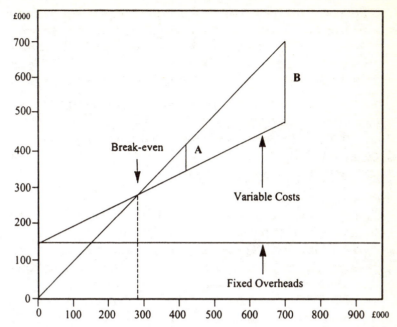

Figure 4.2 *Lower break-even point from reduced fixed overheads*

How was it done?

- The direct material costs (already variable) were renegotiated on favourable terms leading also to the loss of the publicity manager (a removal of a fixed cost upon changing a variable).
- The direct labour costs before the reorganization were really semi-variable in nature. After reorganization they became truly 'variable'. The indirect workers and the supervisors, previously fixed costs, were successfully converted to variable.
- The payment method provided an incentive which reduced this variable cost still further for each item packed.
- Part of the 'fixed' remuneration paid to the salesmen was converted to 'variable'.
- A major (fixed) cost was reduced when the warehouse space was used more economically.
- Some fixed costs were removed or reduced, and others were converted to variable on favourable terms.
- This conversion of fixed costs to variable costs had the effect of reducing the gross margin or contribution from 63 per cent to

56 per cent. This was well worthwhile since it was the reduction of the fixed overhead from its previous unacceptable level that did the trick. It is still high by most standards but will reduce still further when normal sales levels are achieved. At sales of £600,000, it will not be very far out.

This example illustrates the possibilities of enhancing business security by converting fixed costs into variable. As in the example, an examination of these possibilities often results in the straightforward removal or reduction of fixed overheads outright. No overhead is 'fixed' in the last resort.

Subcontract

All business activities are regarded in a fresh light and their cost is compared with that of subcontracting them to third parties. The converse is also true. Those items already in the hands of third parties are examined with a view to bringing them in-house provided the quality and cost savings can justify the step.

It is a question of each to his own forte. You may be attempting to provide a function internally when others outside have by far the greater experience or scale benefits to offer it more cheaply.

It is all too easy to be led by 'status' implications or make investments 'cart-before-horse'. You may in consequence have dedicated a whole factory and its attendant overheads to providing a product or service before you have built up sufficient retail sales volumes. Sometimes regarded as 'planning for the future', untimely investment in this kind of operation can be suicidal when good alternative subcontract facilities exist at keen prices. If you have to do so, better to start under the railway arches than in prestigious premises that absorb all your capital or send borrowings through the roof.

Selectivity

This involves pruning out unprofitable activities, not simply at the more obvious contribution level or gross margin, but after a thorough analysis of all company overheads attributable to each product or branch.

Efficiency improvements

As the name implies all aspects of running the business are scrutinized in a drive to improve general efficiency in all areas.

You might look for rationalization possibilties. Remember that fixing a limited number of standard end products does not amount to a full rationalization process. This is only achieved when you keep standardized sub-assemblies in hand that can be fitted into a range of end products (as in the Meccano principle).

Incentives
An attempt is made to improve performance by introducing or changing financial and other incentives. Schemes sometimes become stale and a better response is obtained simply by the change alone.

Spending to save
Major savings can sometimes be established by a minimal outlay in one area or another. On a larger scale, an expensive advertising campaign can gear up the size of the business if the risk can be taken.

Fine tuning
There are times when an operation has a good product and reputation in the market and yet fails to convert the advantage to profits. This can result from woolly thinking and be overcome by quite simple fine tuning. The whole business profile must first be examined before the obvious is revealed.

Early in his career the author joined such an enterprise in the capacity of finance director of a sub-group of an international plc.

The operation had moved from congested premises in London to the south, seduced by financial incentives to move into a modern, spacious factory. Assistance was given with housing also and the morale was good. The firm was about 100 years old and its prestigious products enjoyed 75 per cent market share. It also possessed the Royal Warrant.

Nevertheless, the industry was quite small and the concern employed 100 direct workers (manufacturing boilers and ancillary equipment), an equal number in the field servicing the many boilers that had been sold over the years, and the usual proportion of indirect workers and staff.

When quoting for complete kitchen installations it used competitors' products in certain areas to complement its own.

A complete kitchen for the catering industry could cost up to the equivalent today of £2 million for a single large installation. However, most of the sales were made up of piecemeal items such as individual boilers, coffee machines, stainless steel countering and so on. There was also a development company selling coffee services to offices and using a machine, made within the group as part of the service, on free loan. This made a good margin and was secured by taking a deposit against the safe return of the machine. This, and an advance payment for the final coffee pack on withdrawal, helped to finance the operation. This all sounds very well but what was wrong?

It had a turnover equivalent to £30 million, the lion's share of its market, a good product and reasonable margins on its sales. Why did it constantly embarrass itself by failing to meet a very low profit budget?

None of the answers were revolutionary. The steps taken to correct the situation at best could only be described as fine tuning. These were the problems:

- The management could not believe its bad luck each time the accounts were produced. Was it an accountant's curse? Woolly thinking prevailed where strategic planning was wanting.
- The firm was ambitious and had made it a priority to win the remaining small share of their boiler market predominantly in the north. In anticipation of this expansion in market share the annual budget contained a growth factor of some 6 or 7 per cent.
- The budget also provided for the full complement of kitchen design staff and works personnel to handle this business. There was a bit of good old-fashioned 'empire building' going on, but the work never arrived.
- This was not because prices were too high. In fact they had been frozen for two years (despite inflation) in an effort to corner the trade, but the publicity had failed to get the message across.
- The pioneer coffee service company had shown no profit even though there had been rapid sales growth. There were too many cancelled contracts, heavy marketing costs, and a

number of inefficient salesmen (some of whom were dishonest).

- The accounts that were prepared hid more than they revealed:
  1. Nobody knew fully who was responsible for what
  2. Profit centres were geographically based by major city. The coffee operation aside, they were all inclusive of manufacturing, factored sales and service and spares activities. Among other things, this concealed the large loss in the service activities.
  3. Debtor collection was very weak and interest costs were severe.

Every year the plans had been similar – provision for expansion with attendant overheads – non-delivery and perpetuation into the following year. You could not see the wood for the trees. There was plenty of scope in the very next budget presented to the parent board. It included the following departures from previous practice:

Strategic

- A market growth rate of only 2 per cent was assumed, in line with past experience.
- The excess built-in overhead was stripped out (this was not difficult because it had never been called upon).
- Price increases were implimented sufficient to make up the inflation arrears and allow for the current year in advance. Margins were much enhanced.
- The prices in the service division were raised further. Spare part prices were especially loaded, and a better deal on annual maintenance contracts was introduced as an alternative to casual service charges to attract cash up front. This also halved the paperwork.
- Payments to service engineers were strictly restricted for unexplained or excessive lost time on the road or whatever.
- The dead wood was removed from the coffee plan. Further investment in growth was held back for a short period in return for quality. The sales were there and now profits could show through. The team could begin to believe in its future.

Accounting
- Responsibility accounting was introduced.
- Proper product and service divisions were created.
- The debtor arrears were eradicated with the help of computerization.

Management
- Adverse variances from budget were at once identified and compensatory action was taken.
- Fresh investment was now directed to lowest risk highest return projects. Those which could be taken quickly with fewest problems were ranked first.

The result

Nothing in the plan was revolutionary. The turnover was little different, the products the same. The company for the first time slightly exceeded its budget much to the surprise and relief of the main board.

It went on to double its profits in each of the next five years and eventually became the group's largest profit earner! It was also the most liquid!

This one time somewhat disregarded subsidiary among 80 others, now held centre stage. (The coffee service company helped to convert the nation to coffee and Kenco into the nation's largest coffee importer.)

This goes to show that attention to detail and a little fine tuning can go a long way. It does not always have to be drastic and sometimes stares you in the face. Once achieved, success can go on breeding success as was the case in the example given.

Swinging the axe

We are now entering more brutal territory, often in the hands of outsiders.

The economic recession, dilution of union power and increased management strength have all given the means and impetus to those whose job it is to roll heads immediately upon appointment, be they internal or appointed from outside. You do need a certain personality and attitude to carry out this task successfully.

Quick to spot non-strategic, overmanned areas, the experts have no time for long sophisticated analysis. Panic is the order of the day since the business will usually die unless the bleeding is stopped at once.

Shedding payroll costs is the most certain and immediate method of providing temporary security while the longer-term trading requisites have to take second place. You won't find this approached very scientifically. There will be a minimum target of £X to be removed from the payroll or whichever expense source.

The axeman will usually identify his targets based initially on past experience, and the need to move quickly. If he is new to the company he may face advice or strong resistance from the established management team.

That being the case, it is a common ploy to quantify the value to be removed by each department head within a short time. If recommendations that match his requirement are not forth-coming then the action continues without the benefit of the management input.

If the action is too crude it can trigger the 'self-destruct mode' already discussed. If the patient is likely to die anyway, the justification for doing something is clear for all to see.

Summary

The concept of 'swinging the axe' is to take a quantum sum out of total costs – usually manning – sufficient to stem a net cash outflow in the shortest possible time.

It can self-destruct but is seen as the only alternative and is not meant to be particularly scientific. Long-term facilities will be sacrificed without doubt but its prime aim is to make sure that there will be a future.

Reaction management

We discussed the principles of reaction managment earlier and explained the dangers of its use to the exclusion of proper forward planning. It has its place as a fire-fighting device until sudden severe difficulties are reversed.

If it is used as a normal routine the management will not look ahead, but wait for the crises to manifest themselves first. Such a practice is at best haphazard and unco-ordinated. It amounts to little better than a goal-keeper mentality, and at worst is likely to run into serious difficulty sooner or later for the reasons we have discussed.

There were at one time several sizeable groups trading independently within the mass manufacturing end of the ophthalmic industry in Britain. After the First World War the product was classified as being of military importance, and certain foreign firms were invited to leave the country. The British company taking their place had gone through some bad times, but after some attention began to expand rapidly through acquisition until it became a virtual monopoly and second to none on the world stage.

A league table of the largest 2,000 companies was compiled by a well-known, reputable organization, and the group took thirty-fourth place. It also took first place in a competition based on the standard and content of its annual accounts.

To win the exalted league table position it had to be shown that its profits had progressively increased without hiccup for a number of years (12 in this case) and cash flow was the next important of three criteria. There were enough accolades to leave the management a little complacent about its success, and all achieved by effective reaction to opportunities as they arose. You could say this was the plus side. What could go wrong? The answer – plenty!

First the exalted league table position failed the group because it was based on poorly judged premisses. Much of the profit growth had been the result of acquisitions and not organic growth. Prudent provision in difficult years had helped to smooth the effect of fluctuations.

The cash flow projection measured prospective cash flow, that is to say calculated profits plus depreciation (being a non-cash item). It had no regard to the cash that was spent or was to pour into stocks later. The third criterion was a derivative of the others.

It was difficult to see why so much investment was going into glass ophthalmic lenses simply because they had been the fashion of the past. All the grinding, smoothing and polishing of glass lenses, and the attendant equipment, had to be seen to be believed. It is true to say that early attempts to interest the public in plastic lenses had been badly received because of scratching problems which had not been alleviated. It was the strong opinion of the group that sand-based glass would always be a cheaper alternative to oil-based plastic, and there was very limited demand anyway.

Short-term considerations always prevail when cohesive long-term planning is scorned. Alternatives are not properly considered and all aspects of the business are not brought together for examination as a cohesive whole. Half-yearly profit statements concentrate most of management's time and the resultant effect on the share price.

Flirtations with Pilkington resulted eventually in an unwelcome public take-over bid. Long-term planning may have been eschewed but this really focused the mind on short-term defence needs. The Office of Fair Trading was involved, a full take-over defence launched, and it all ended up in front of the Monopolies and Mergers Commission.

Dividend control was in force at the time. This had had the effect of depressing the group's share price because the profits shown, and retained in the business, could not be paid to the shareholders at a commercial rate.

Perhaps this was just as well considering that the profits on which the group had been judged were not matched with any real cash generation. The legislation permitted companies to raise their dividend in such circumstances as part of their take-over defence. Of necessity now this was dictated by short-term considerations and the raised dividend was supported by a higher profit forecast. The day-to-day running of the business was forced into second place in an effort to retain independence.

It was during this period that an American manufacturing base in Wales had come on to the market. To buy it would give the group a total monopoly, but to leave it might incite Japanese intentions or suck in imports. The Monopolies and Mergers Commission ruled that a horizontal integration could take place, notwithstanding that the vertical integration attempt by Pilkington was being fiercely fought off, on grounds of diminished efficiency. Other things were stirring, however.

The Americans had successfully imposed statutory regulations aimed at protecting their industry from imports. This related to the safety thickness of the lens at the centre, and the base curves on which they were manufactured. This made glass lenses even heavier and encouraged an unprecedented increase in the sale of plastic lenses – now enjoying better success with scratch-resistant processes. Plastic moulded lenses were in the pipeline.

The world was moving into recession, and the total market was shrinking. Around the world, firms started to take their export sales much more seriously, and 'hands off' agreements were discarded in a free-for-all. It led one leading American company to quit the industry in favour of promoting its contact lenses, and its glass ophthalmic lens stocks flooded the world for two years or more.

The British firm won its contest with Pilkington and now fixed its attention on meeting the all-important profit forecast. This was met, but the cupboard was bare.

The plastic lens market was to grow to some 50 per cent in many countries (more in some). The shrinking glass lens market was hit twice: once by recession and again by plastic lens growth. The company in question had not planned ahead or seen the signs that were there, or the inevitable. Surely the fact that the Americans were keen to shed their UK glass plant should have been a clue to what was happening?

Still money was being pumped into glass lens stocks and machinery alike. It was even argued that the cost of investing in stock was efficient because the net of tax cost was cheaper than it would be after tomorrow's inflation. And then spectacle lenses are beyond obsolescence risks are they not?

Interest rates were abnormally low at the time relative to inflation – but could it last? The business was running further out of control. Stocks were being returned from the warehouses to the producing factories.

The 'paper' results recorded during the past years had benefited greatly from the factory overhead element of production taken into profit. To disgorge stocks now, even to limit production, would have the opposite effect just at the time when the group did not want to fall flat on its face after meeting the profit forecast. The cost of financing ever-mounting stocks, the cost of the misdirected investment and the higher dividend commitment were now imposing an enormous strain on resources. Caught 'with their trousers down', interest rates doubled.

A few years earlier gearing had been almost zero following a rights issue but it was now high, yet the board were still enjoying the accolades attaching to their ever-rising profit trend. So too for that matter was the City.

Following a terse board meeting, announcements were made that two plants would be closed immediately and major redundancies initiated elsewhere. Back to more reaction management.

To de-stock in a shrinking market meant that production had to be run at a mere fraction of total capacity. This led to:

- Loss of production overhead recovered in profits
- Reversal of previous recoveries on the stocks shed
- Plants running at inefficient levels relative to volumes and indivisible costs
- Substantial costs of redundancies and closures.

The result?
The group recorded its first ever loss and the share price plummeted. Paradoxically, this was its best year ever in genuine cash flow.

Having taken its medicine the group traded on with a much meaner cost base and recovered to the extent necessary to support its sale at the first decent opportunity. It was the attraction of its catering equipment sub-group that made the deal possible rather than the ophthalmic activities which were sold on again after purchase.

The lesson
This example shows how a firm can be mauled by one crisis after another by reaction management doctrines that do not put management in the driving seat at all.

We have to react to crises and we have to take opportunities as they present themselves. But we don't have to make a habit of reaction management. Do not be a business of last resort cures.

The complete rebuild
There are some entities that would consider all the techniques so far discussed 'child's play'. Some are asset strippers, purely and simply. Others act strongly with urgency to ensure that their returns are maximized as soon as possible. Sometimes it is the very

threat of failure that spurs them on to greater achievements, especially if they are responsible for an acquired company.

The action is often more violent than the axeman techniques. On day one after the acquisition is made a whole 'hit squad' may descend on the target from head office. It's purpose? – The complete rebuild.

This technique involves the closest possible examination of the business from top to bottom. Options to sell, dissect or close down each product or part of the business are considered one by one in the most minute detail.

Realizable values will be taken if they are greater than trading returns, but after first considering key customer relationships. Exit costs and final windfall profit opportunities will be considered in the equation, and absolutely nothing is regarded as 'fixed'. Indeed, the word will be banned from use as are the words 'marginal' and 'contribution'. Product profitability assessments are taken right to the 'bottom line' in each individual case.

Activity is sifted according to product, then to the machines used and the space occupied. Machines or space attracting little profitable activity are carefully noted.

The same attention is focused on the balance sheet as well as all revenue areas. As each product or activity is taken out of the worksheets the result is analysed, products reintroduced and sifted through time and time again in all possible combinations. The theory will each time be tested against the practical possibilities, and a view taken whether each cost allocated to a product can indeed be removed.

All possible company profiles are considered until one is found that maximizes the return on capital employed. This will start with the analysis of closedown or sale prospects of the total operation. It will then progress to a consideration of partial disposals, the unlikely extreme at the other end being to take no action whatever. Everything possible is considered to bend the firm into the desirable shape.

The return on capital employed is reviewed after each profile is completed.

Key customers, employees and suppliers will be kept informed as appropriate. Customers may be recommended to place final stock orders for withdrawn goods, or be informed that substantial price increases must be imposed on pain of withdrawal. They may be informed that supply will continue provided that the customer does not double-source and gives the firm the benefit of all its business. There will be exit profits to be taken as well as the cost of redundancies and closures to be met.

Eventually, everything will fall into place and a decision will be taken to:

- Dispose of the business for value
- Close it down
- Continue to run it in changed form
- Prune out the main profit and shoe-horn it into a smaller space
- Prune it and append it to another group operation.

In practice, the 'stay as you are' alternative is not on the agenda. The name of the game is to improve the situation and reputations are at stake.

The implementation may be complicated and phased so that redundancy arrangements can be fixed some time in advance, the employees being paid a premium for their continuing cooperation.

The action is often imposed from outside. One company very active in this field uses a much acclaimed 'hit squad' which descends upon the victim in a line of black BMWs to impose maximum terror. The use of such cars is banned to others in the operation. For good measure they will dispose of some or all of the existing directors almost immediately, and this soon establishes a status quo. Their arrival signals that things will never be the same again.

Guilty or otherwise, the old management team are treated with contempt. They will not lead in the decisions that follow and, deprived of all motivation, they will give way to newly charged managers in due course selected by the hit squad.

The ultimate solution will be given the blessing of the main board and then the action will commence in earnest. In the long run it will make economic sense and ensure the most efficient use of the assets in the business. Almost immediately the hit squad will be on its way to its next target, the new management in place freshly motivated and not tarnished by the upheaval that has gone on before. This approach to regenerating a business is the most dramatic of all the concepts discussed here.

It is top league and may serve to make you look at your business with fresh eyes.

The roles of management

It is important that the management team should be fully briefed regarding the problem, if any, and the task in hand.

They should be united by the common purpose, by the style and manner of the chief executive who should convene a meeting at the outset, and further meetings as the exercise progresses. These meetings should be single purpose and exclude other day-to-day matters unless strictly relevant. Otherwise the important central issue will be lost among the other discussion.

The chief executive will set the level of urgency and the general tone. Each manager will be responsible for making his staff conscious of the requirements of their department.

Apart from contributing to the general debate each manager will be asked to make recommendations in his own area of responsibility. If savings are essential the meeting will try to agree how much must be forthcoming from each area. The managers will then be given a certain time, not too long, to match the requirement with specific suggestions.

If they fail to meet the target action may be imposed.

What do we do first?

Hopefully, there will be no need to act except for the odd opportunity recognized here or there.

There may be a problem of more or less magnitude which we should now contemplate. This could always arise in the future if circumstances beyond our control turn against us.

If there is a crisis it is good practice to call a general meeting of all employees to inform them of the problem and ask for their cooperation. Give them all the assurances that you are able to and any bright news on the horizon that they may not have heard.

If you do this at the outset there is a much better chance that you will win their support. If there is a problem they will be more conscious of the signs than you think, and the meeting will help to relieve tensions and clear the air.

When all is done those that remain with the company will be more than thankful that the action has rescued the business and at least, for the moment, secured their jobs.

Just when you are dreading how dismissals may be received you may well find that you are hailed as a hero rather than the villain.

First aid
Some first aid may be called for. If you can immediately identify the initial steps that can be taken without undue harm, now is the time to act. It will give you a breathing space and impact straight away on your cash flow. You could be buying valuable time without which other action would be too late.

Remember that the first priority must be to stem the bleeding. If you do no more than eliminate an adverse cash flow you will survive to tend to your longer-term health needs.

Finding the hard core profit
Decide which activities and products are generating sound margins and profits. Most businesses have a hard core activity that stands out above the others in terms of its value and profitability.

Identify it and the minimum employee structure that is required to secure its future. Until you decide otherwise all other activity is suspect. Companies often get into trouble because they have strayed too far from this hard core activity in the first place. Some widen their range so they can argue that it is fully comprehensive. It may be the fringe items that are causing the problem.

How to recognize lost causes and mistakes
Considerable sums may have been ploughed into a project, and reputations may be at stake. Conduct a thorough search for all such candidates and take an honest, pragmatic view of their chances.

Ultimate future success may not be enough to compensate for the further monies and the time and effort that will be expended now.

It is not a competition, and you do not have to prove yourself to those who are working with you towards a common aim. That purpose is the return on the business and its stability.

If your cash position dictates it even the best causes will have to go if you are to survive. Certainly look for all alternatives, or try to hold the project on the shelf where it may possibly be resurrected later.

Mistakes are made in every business and you are entitled to yours. If there is a problem you must now recognize lost causes and mistakes, and you will be better respected if you do. Step back and ask yourself what is the alternative to the action now proposed. If that is unthinkable you have no choice.

When you have taken the requisite action do not day dream about what might have been, or indulge in recriminations. This will only detract from the task in hand and the business must go on. Other jobs are at stake.

What stays – what goes?

You will have used one of the techniques we have discussed to draw up a hit list for action. Write each item down and add any further indirect or less obvious financial benefits. An example might be the national insurance that you pay in addition to salaries, or it might be the reduction in petrol costs or machine maintenance.

Check that the total meets the target that you set yourself and that you are not removing any item that is interdependent with those that you are keeping.

In other words, pore over the list very carefully to ensure that it is entirely practical, and remember the special position of key customers. If your intended action is likely to affect their supplies, you will keep their goodwill if you visit them first to explain your plans. Give them the opportunity to place any final top-up orders for goods or spare parts until they find another source.

If the product margin is the problem you may do well to suggest that a serious price increase could avert the need to cut lines. However, you may lock yourself into a situation in doing so that will not give you any long-term benefit if cheaper competing products are available.

Who stays – who goes?

This will be the hardest part of all, save for any trouble makers that you may be pleased to dispense with.

Employees may include friends and relatives, or people you have encountered every day for many years. Any redundancies are bound to cause hardship. You will have to ensure that the complement that stay have all the necessary matching skills to carry on the business. Think of each vital skill area and discipline and consider how well covered it will remain after the action.

You have to be tough in business whether you find this easy or not. You also have to remain the good guy to your department or your company.

Your department should be the decision-making forum. The finance director will provide the management team with the analysis that will influence your decisions, and it should be the task of the personnel manager or director (or equivalent) to carry them out. As a manager, it is a mistake to attempt all three functions yourself unless you place particular value on face-to-face confrontations and can trust your own financial skills. That may well be your own particular discipline.

If the business cannot survive without loss of jobs rest your conscience in the knowledge that you have saved the positions that remain, along with the company.

New blood?

This is a convenient time to consider whether each member of the management team is performing well. Some will be bruised and blunted by the action that is being carried out, and their enthusiasm may never be the same again.

You may have exposed some weaknesses in skills and experience in certain areas which could be filled by a change or additional new blood. Think through this carefully and act accordingly.

The action programme

Having agreed any necessary action, the management team should now draw up a full programme.

This will include all the steps from start to finish, the target dates in each case and the initials of the person or persons delegated to the task.

The following examples are indicative although by no means exhaustive:

Submit new price details to printers	May 1	RLS
Circulate price announcement to customers	7	RLS
Meeting of employees to explain actions	8	FTG

Visit major debtors to collect cheques	8	SLB
Issue redundancy notices	9	PJW
Release prepared press statement if a public company and the action is significant	9	JFG
Clear out obsolete plant and stocks	11	DWF
Meeting with landlord to negotiate lease surrender and revised requirements	14	JFG
Clear offices vacated by redundant staff	15	RCC
Paint reception area	15	ITT
Progress review meeting	16	ALL
Calculate final pay packages	17	DEG
Appoint sub-committee to follow up new technology and make proposals	18	JFG
Meeting with bank to explain position, action taken and new prospects	18	CMG
Issue newsletter to all employees retained	24	JIG
Receive and check first consignment of cheaper materials already ordered	26	MNN
Board meeting	31	ALL

Everything will be double checked to ensure that there are no important omissions and that legislative procedures are being fully complied with.

This agreed, the chief executive will monitor day-by-day progress and deal with any unexpected difficulties as they arise.

Avoiding self-destruction

The risks of having to take very severe action have already been discussed. We concluded that it is possible to lose customer confidence and orders to the point where the remaining business is not sufficient to support the retained staff. This can take us back to square one when further action causes the firm to fall apart.

The first rule in avoiding this dramatic kind of self-destruction is to ensure that the management team observes strict rules regarding the confidential information with which they are entrusted. The same applies to others to whom tasks are delegated.

Outsiders will be curious. Brief your telephone operator well and others in close contact with outside parties.

Select one spokesperson to take any press calls. Ensure that no such calls are put through to anyone else and that the person selected to deal with them is working from a prepared brief. He should not feel that he has to answer any questions that are not within the brief and he may require tenacity to avoid being led into statements he does not want to make.

This applies particularly with public companies where a bad or misleading media report can immediately impact on the share price. There is no shame in sticking to the lines of the prepared statement and insisting that there is nothing further that the company wishes to say at the moment.

Do not let the Press attribute any statements to you personally unless you are briefed to do so for policy purposes, but be prepared for the difficult character who will do so whatever you say.

Do not act until you are ready, but then do so swiftly and cleanly with no last minute prevarication. Redundancies cause very mixed emotions affecting both those going and those staying. Be as fair with them as you can and remember that any ill treatment now will cause bad feeling that will carry into the future. When it comes to the day for their departure this is best just before a weekend or a holiday. The break helps everybody to absorb the events before work recommences and others seek fresh employment.

If the action contemplated is very dramatic you may wish to avoid the worst effects by splitting it into two or three tranches. The downside is that the threat will be hanging over employees for a longer period when morale will be very low.

Sometimes, however, it sorts out those with less commitment to the business who then leave of their own accord. It is also always possible to give all the affected employees notice of your future intentions if you pay them extra for their cooperation in making it a smooth and more gradual transition as we saw in the 'complete rebuild' example.

This way the business may absorb the shock waves rather better. You may decide to visit your major customers and suppliers to allay unfounded fears before any problems start. If desirable, use another pretext for the visit and adopt a natural but sincere approach.

It will all depend upon the circumstances in each case and is a matter for your judgement.

The business plan

Establishing the business plan

Now is the time to view the result and give fresh impetus by establishing the *business plan*.

The hard work has been largely completed. To establish our business plan we refer once again to the inertia forecast that we have already prepared. This will already be in the format that we require for our business plan.

The first task is to amend the inertia forecast in all respects for the action that we have now taken or set in motion. False aspirations must be excluded. Any changes that have taken place between first compiling the forecast and the present time must also be introduced.

A business plan, like an annual budget, must be one that we can accomplish with a reasonable level of certainty. It is after all a plan, not some hopeful target which we will never attain. It will form the backbone of everything we do next from manning plans through to product marketing and advertising.

We will need to check thoroughly that it contains no errors, double counting or inconsistencies. It will help if we evaluate the changes that have taken place and check that the planned result has been improved to the same extent. It still has to be accomplished but it must be accurate in the first place.

Some of our changes will have had an indirect effect on other areas such as working capital usage, depreciation charges and interest. These you may have overlooked and you will now work through them to ensure that they all make sense.

You will want to know that the end result measures up to all your expectations and requirements (in so far as it is in your power to do so) in terms of return on capital, the various health check criteria and cash headroom.

The business plan may point to matters that are outstanding and still require attention. Quite the most important may indeed be the need to improve your cash headroom.

What will a good business plan contain?

The answer to this question will help to explain what is also required of a good inertia forecast, or the annual budget and accounts reports. They are drawn up for separate purposes over different periods but many of the features are the same.

The business plan should have the following essential ingredients:

- Front summary of the most crucial information only
- A summary of those health checks that can be built into the computer model (much harder for manual plans) shown in contrast with well-accepted standards from industry and the banking community
- A capital employed statement
- A summary trading account and profit and loss account
- Detailed backing sheets showing all revenues and costs in suitable departments and functions along the lines incorporated in your monthly accounts. Responsibilities of different managers should be kept to separate sheets and summary totals if at all possible.
- A cash flow statement showing all funds required, their method of finance and the net funds generated or used
- A cash facilities statement showing ageing, new lines, repayment tranches and headroom against usage. It should also show the headroom left against any imposed borrowing limitations
- Manning details in summary form by department and date
- A shareholding statement from which any fresh issues can be calculated and introduced into the cash flow statement.

A summary and proof of the interest calculation may also be useful to you although this will not be intended for circulation. Also useful will be a taxation summary prepared by yourselves or your accountants.

Sensitivity and probability

The top management should also equip themselves with a statement which summarizes the effects of sensitivity along the lines discussed earlier when preparing spreadsheets. The major advantage of a well-designed business plan, held on a computer, is that you can play an infinite number of tunes on it.

If you want to know the bottom line effect on profits, say of achieving 3 per cent more sales than plan, you can key in this single change and the program should be capable of amending all the affected figures in an instant.

There can of course only be one business plan or it is not worth the paper it is written on. It may be revised from time to time but even this temptation may make you lose the way. The fewer changes the better. If at all possible take appropriate action to get back on course before you change the plan which you are all working to achieve.

Returning to the question of sensitivity it is still invaluable to know the effects on the plan of a range of variable conditions that you are most likely to encounter.

These should be calculated by use of the model in steps of 1 per cent at a time. If you know the result of a 1 per cent change it is a simple matter to gross this up by further multiples of 1 per cent to reflect any greater change.

The most common areas which you should test are:

- Sales volume changes
- Price increases
- Interest rates
- Inflation
- Driving factors such as population if the effect is sufficiently close
- Limiting factors if they have direct impact.

There are many more that you may think of which are relevant to your business. After the first four traditional areas they tend to become more subjective and less valuable, however.

This is not in any way decrying the value of this important exercise. To know the first four, in particular, will show you the results of minor changes in the most sensitive areas you will meet in practice.

This will reveal to you just how sensitive your plan is to matters you must expect to encounter. You will then be left considering the *probabilities* of these variations occurring in practice. You should never accept the first business plan which is prepared. It would be a miracle if this were at once the right one.

Reinvestment

If the result of the exercise has been at all traumatic you will want to preserve the future security of the business.

Such times of review often present the best opportunities for reinvestments in plant and machinery, techniques, product selection and design which will give you the head start you need to beat off the competition and win.

You will be concentrating on throwing out the unwanted elements and building on the profitable hard core products. You may well be suddenly cash rich as a result of the actions you have taken, or you may be on the point of refinancing the enterprise through fresh shareholder, banking, or other funds.

If you can now reinvest to make your retained products the best in the market, unassailable to attack, you will have achieved a great deal.

Selling the plan to employees

You now have a plan to sell. There may be unpalatable parts in it that employees will not like but you will have an opportunity also to give them the good news.

You will have to prepare what to say and the management team should play a role in assisting you. It will be best to call a meeting especially for the purpose.

This will be the very best opportunity to reunite all employees and create a new atmosphere and a fresh motivation.

If your actions can be seen to be making general commercial sense you will most likely be forgiven for the parts that are less welcome. Your skills in securing the health of the business and safeguarding your employees' source of income will be recognized.

All will see that you have your finger on the pulse and this alone will generate a feeling of better security. It is a task that you should look forward to. Tackle it in this frame of mind, however difficult it may be.

5

Providing the Finance

The basic alternatives

The main sources of finance for a business will normally fall within one of the following categories:

1. Shareholders
2. Retained reserves
3. Debenture holders
4. Government-sponsored schemes and venture capital
5. Joint ventures and partnerships
6. Development capital
7. Acceptance credits
8. Trade debts
9. Bills of exchange
10. Factoring debts
11. Inter-company loans
12. Financial institutions and private financiers
13. Finance in kind
14. Tax provisions
15. Hire purchase, renting and leasing agreements
16. Banks.

Shareholders

The original shareholders will have invested in the business at the outset and will be the holders of ordinary share capital. Subsequently, sometimes simultaneously, other special rights and classes of shares may have arisen.

Shares are sometimes issued by tender. This will apply especially to public sector services which are subsequently privatized.

Invitations to tender are advertised in the press and by television and a form is provided for the purpose. In the event of over-subscription the allocation of shares is reduced to those that have tendered on a pro rata basis.

Developing private businesses are often converted into public companies when the shares can be dealt in more freely. As needs arise the current shareholders may be approached to honour calls on previous undertakings already given, or they may be invited to subscribe for new capital on a pro rata basis. These 'rights issues' are a common method of raising capital for expanding companies.

Other similar variations may include the issue of bonus shares, shares in lieu of dividend or special placements of shares from new sources and backed by underwriters.

The shares may be issued at their nominal value or at a premium in which case the premium remains locked in as part of the shareholders' funds in the company. In some countries the banks invest directly into the equity of business and take a share.

Retained reserves

Profits earned but not distributed as dividends to shareholders remain in the company in the form of reserves which help to finance the capital employed and future operations. They may also include certain other non-distributable windfalls or gains usually of a capital nature.

Debenture holders

Debentures holders, unlike shareholders, are not the owners of the company. They advance long-term loans which will be secured against specific assets or they will take a general floating charge on all the assets of the company. In the event of a failure to observe the terms of the debenture deed they usually obtain special further rights which may then include voting rights.

Some classes of debenture take a lower return but the holders are entitled to convert them into share capital before a given date in return for a premium on the share price at the time of issue of the debentures.

Loan capital obtained through debentures goes in and out of fashion according to the taxation rules and other alternatives at the time.

Government-sponsored schemes and venture capital

Such schemes are often run by the banks on behalf of the government which determines the rules.

Their purpose is to serve as an incentive to encourage new businesses to get off the ground. They will consist of loans which contain certain concessions according to the scheme currently in force. They are aimed at encouraging small start-up business situations for the most part, but are not normally awarded without adequate security.

Joint ventures and partnerships

Existing companies may combine their financial resources to back a commercial venture in which they are both interested. There may be more than two participants, as is often the case in some of the major projects which have been financed this way, requiring technology from different sources and huge sums of money.

Each business may pledge itself to inject so much cash into the enterprise to support it as it proceeds, or the assistance may take the form of providing goods or services. These can all be accounted for on an informal basis without the issue of any capital, or a formal joint venture company may be formed for the purpose.

Partnerships of professional people are conducted on similar lines and the method is open to those to whom the advantages of limited liability are not strictly relevant.

Development capital

Development capital may come from private sources or from financial institutions, trusts and the like with available monies to invest.

The markets will serve to introduce companies requiring support and those looking for an opportunity to obtain a significant share in an expanding business or in a rescue situation.

Management buy-outs are commonly financed in this manner and it is an industry all of its own. The development capital company may be an equity holding division of a major bank or one set up to specialize in its own right.

A management team will receive the backing of this organization to negotiate with the existing shareholders to take the business over. They will be supported in the belief that they will accomplish much more than the previous shareholders.

Once the acquisition is completed the development company will take the minority shareholding, leaving the majority with the buy-out team by way of incentive. The financiers will commonly fix a target date by when the firm will have succeeded sufficiently in its profit record to 'go public'. This will be the opportunity for them to take their windfall capital return, but if the target performance is not met they will obtain progressively increasing dividend and shareholding rights in lieu.

In this case the buy-out team will only be expected to subscribe 'hurt money' by way of capital in the venture. This will be sufficiently significant to them for it to hurt in the event of failure. They are therefore encouraged positively by the high rewards if they succeed and the threat of losing more than this if they fail.

Such teams are those normally involved in the management of the company, not being the owners, at the time. They will be complemented by people who can fill the gap for any missing skills.

Other variations include freelance teams of managers who can obtain support to 'buy in' to businesses where they have played no previous role. There are marauding teams of such business managers that combine to seek out opportunities where they can obtain entry to companies that are seen to be performing below par.

More complicated forms of finance include arrangements where a lender will take an equity share in the company, but where the borrower will have the right within a certain time to buy back the shares at a premium as compensation to the lender. The equity arm of a bank may be prepared to provide this form of finance if it is keen to support the company, and other potential business is on the line.

Acceptance credits

These instruments are obtained through discount houses and the banks. A short-term loan is obtained for up to 12 months, often at keen rates of interest, depending on central bank and government activity in the discount house market.

It is a method available to industry of obtaining short-term funds on reasonable terms. The interest is usually paid 'up-front' so that the recipient receives the net funds after interest and is responsible for repaying the gross amount of the advance at the maturity date.

Trade debts

Monies owed to creditors form part of the short-term finance to businesses. Goods and services are normally supplied on credit so that the advantage of holding them is enjoyed in advance of the date when payment is due. This therefore constitutes a form of short-term finance on the balance sheet.

It is often the case that businesses are late in paying their bills as a deliberate policy. This practice can be quite infuriating to the supplier who ends up financing his customer. If he has a particular interest in doing so, however, he may allow the debt to roll up in return for conversion rights into equity in agreed circumstances.

From time to time all businesses and industries encounter recessions, over-capacity in the product or similar circumstances which make sales very hard to obtain. In these conditions it is not at all uncommon for sales representatives to be allowed to offer very attractive extended credit terms. It is reasoned that it is better to obtain a sale on these conditions than merely to leave the stock on the shelf. Normal trade credit of one month is typically extended by anything up to 12 months in such difficult times.

This opportunity is available to the purchaser. We now look at some examples open to the seller.

Bills of exchange

Export business can be more volatile than trade in the home market. It is therefore usually conducted by some secure means, the paperwork releasing the goods being preceded by that securing payment. There is a range of methods open to the selling company if local customs permit and the purchaser can be persuaded to conform.

A regular method involves the use of bills of exchange, a negotiable instrument which can be signed on to other parties in return for cash 'up front'.

Credit in export markets is usually longer than that awarded in the home market, commonly three, six or sometimes as long as 12 months for normal purposes.

Holders of instruments such as bills of exchange therefore have to wait some time for their money unless they surrender title in return for a reduced sum. The transaction will be subject to appropriate security, recourse or compensation should the purchaser fail in his obligation to pay on the due date.

Factoring debts

There is also a market through which routine home debtors can be assigned to factoring houses in advance of the normal due date for receipt of the funds.

The charge for this service will include an interest element, a collection service charge (if left to the credit control function within the factoring company) and an element of profit. There may also be a credit insurance premium if one or other of the parties wishes to pass the risk to the insurance market. The funds will be advanced net of the charges described, with or without recourse according to the terms.

Inter-company loans

It is common within a group or consortium of companies for those that are in funds to help in the finance of those that are not so well placed. This may be by way of a formal loan document (which is often preferred to overcome legal and taxation problems) or informally. The advance may be left at the discretion of the senior management or written for a specific term, and may be with or without interest.

Usually, any surplus funds are routed to the parent company at the top of the organization. Their reallocation to subsidiary companies will be under the control of the treasurer or treasury department (which can be an external service). No funds will be passed down unless they can be fully justified on financial evaluation and other criteria.

This means that only the most attractive proposals are likely to be financed in this way, and the discipline helps to maximize the overall performance of the group.

Financial institutions and private financiers

There are a number of financial institutions that will help to finance a business, including individual financiers in their own right.

The terms and methods may be quite varied depending on the deal that can be struck.

Finance in kind
There are many ways in which parties to the arrangement may provide finance in kind.

An example is the rent-free use of a building in return for a later benefit agreed by the parties. This may be an obligation to return the building to a good state of repair, an obligation to buy or a share of future profits.

Some countries find it difficult to trade because of currency and other fiscal restrictions. It is sometimes possible in these cases to find a route through barter trade. You may supply Brazil with office machinery in return for its coffee. One commodity helps to finance the other and business that might otherwise be impossible can be conducted.

Such countries often trade in one of the recognized international currencies rather than their own, particularly where the currency is not free or when inflation is rampant. If you keep an open mind then anything is possible.

Tax provisions
Provisions on a balance sheet recognize obligations which are not currently due. They have the effect of ensuring that funds are retained in the business and can in the interim be regarded as a form of finance. There are other similar examples which may occur to you.

While they can be regarded as a form of finance it is only in the sense that the liability is deferred. In the meantime the funds required to meet the liability will have been absorbed into working capital, or as yet undrawn unless you have been very prudent and created a cash sinking fund for the purpose.

Hire purchase, rental and leasing agreements
These are all methods of financing the fixed assets used in the business when the asset itself represents the security to the lender.

You will be wise to ensure that the asset becomes your own property at the end of the transaction, or can otherwise revert to you for a small consideration. Otherwise you may have to start again, or buy new, when the original asset is still in good working order. Alternatively, you may have to pay out disproportionate charges to the original finance company.

The effective rate of interest that you can pay for this service can be very high. Be certain that you know what this is before you disregard alternative methods of finance.

Some agreements contain benefits that you do not need and should not agree to pay for. For example, you may be financing the purchase of a motor-car fleet by this method. If the agreement provides for repairs, emergency replacement cars following a breakdown or accident and similar avoidable services, you can be certain that you will be paying dearly for them.

Rates will vary according to the proximity of the financing company's year end, and its tax shelter for any capital allowances in being from time to time. Shop around, and you may find that there are better deals to be done.

Do not forget your own taxation position. Go for the scheme that offers you the best value after the taxation treatment is taken into account.

Banks

Banks have a variety of lending devices on offer. The main types of advance are:

- Overdrafts
- Bridging finance
- Loans.

Overdrafts are technically repayable on demand. The amount borrowed will fluctuate according to day-to-day changes in the needs of the customer within the agreed ceiling. The sudden withdrawal of an overdraft facility is usually a sign of serious loss of confidence in the customer, and the most common trigger of liquidations.

In other circumstances the need might be brought about by the bank's own position *vis-à-vis* its lending ratios, or because of a government-imposed credit squeeze.

Bridging finance is used to 'bridge' a funding requirement for a short-term need such as the purchase of a house before the proceeds of the one being sold are available. It helps to smooth the transaction and is advanced against the security of the house or other item being sold. Not all transactions can be synchronized for completion on the same date, and this device fills the gap. The solicitors dealing with the sale will be instructed to account for the proceeds directly to the lending bank.

Loans will be for a fixed amount which will usually be drawn down at one time for a definite forward period. They can be negotiated and left by way of reserve, but you may expect in this case to have to pay a commitment fee to the bank. They can sometimes be drawn down in stages and not all at once.

Their repayment may be in one sum at the end of the term, but it is a normal principle of the banks to insist upon staged repayments commencing after a year or two 'repayment holiday'.

The rate of interest may be fixed throughout the term or it may be varied, in which case it can be expressed as so many percentage points above the 'base rate' or the money market rate (LIBOR in the UK). The interest rate formula can become increasingly more complicated. It may for example be chargeable upon rate fluctuations up to a ceiling only (the 'cap'). There may be a 'cap' and a 'collar', a kind of minimum and maximum formula worked out by both parties to keep risks of fluctuation to the minimum.

Once a contract has been established it may be 'swapped' by introducing a third party to the contract who may not be identified to the original lender. In this case the borrower may have taken a certain view regarding the future behaviour of interest rate patterns, and wish that he had struck a different deal. He may now prefer to make an arrangement which exposes him to rate fluctuations rather than the fixed rate negotiated originally in the belief that rates would fall. If he can find an institution with the opposite view there may be middle ground within which a useful deal can be struck. He will remain the principal party to the loan, but if interest rates behave in a certain way he will be responsible for paying the third party the difference over their formula or vice versa. If he is right in his belief he will still be able to benefit even though he committed himself to the original terms.

Most loans that are on a variable rate basis include provision for 'rolling them over' at fixed intervals of three, six and sometimes 12 months. This can be a fixed formula or one where the customer is given the choice within the periods stated. This serves to roll the lending arrangement forward and take account of interest rate changes in the market. Without this facility a commitment to the interest rate would have to be made by both parties over the whole term of the loan. To make the roll-over periods any shorter would be administratively cumbersome.

Since some loans may extend to anything up to 15 years this method of keeping abreast of interest rate fluctuations is essential, and it also replaces the need (as in the case of overdrafts) of making daily interest calculations. Such long-term loans come close to serving the same role as permanent equity, and you have to have a very good case before they can be obtained.

The periodic roll-overs may be drawn down, if the terms permit, by way of acceptance credits. This way the customer can take advantage of any preferential terms available in the acceptance credit market without disadvantage to the lender.

Another alternative which can be written into a loan is the facility to draw it down in stated currencies other than the home currency. This will be of particular relevance to those who have international trade and other dealings. Multi-currency overdraft facilities may also be obtained, and they help to smooth out currency fluctuations for those businesses that have ongoing income sources in foreign currencies. The liability and the source are 'matched' over time so that the exchange rate exposure is minimized.

Yet a further variation is the deployment of 'futures' and 'interest rate options' where a premium is paid for the right to deal at some future date, but not the obligation. You can even get an option on a 'swap' arrangement and there are other 'hedging' schemes available. Forward rate agreements represent another method of marketing which has entered the money market in order to provide the customer with greater variety and flexibility.

As long as there are two agreeable parties just about any arrangement is possible and the banks and institutions themselves will be willing to explain the alternatives in greater detail.

First identify your need and then discuss how closely this can be met. All these interest rate management techniques will be at the fingertips of your treasurer or external treasury service.

Summary
We have seen that there are a great many methods that can be used to borrow funds. They are not limited to those discussed above and the money market will always be willing to explain what is currently on offer.

A healthy business will have used them to minimize its interest cost, but at the same time giving the greatest possible backing and security that prudence demands.

Which source?

It will be a question for your judgement which source you should use.

You should familiarize yourself with all the alternatives, read the signs in the economy and consider your own particular circumstances and requirements. At no time should you take a gambling position or leave yourself open to risk. To do nothing is the greatest gamble. You do have to exercise judgement and some measure of certainty may be of value to you if the premium is acceptable.

If you leave yourself open to market variations, do so as a matter of policy and not through neglect.

Relationships with bankers and others

We now turn to the special relationships that have to be cultivated and observed between a willing lender and a borrower. The principles apply to all the categories of borrowing which were considered earlier in this chapter.

When you have established the more permanent capital in the business it will be to the traditional bankers that you are most likely to turn for your further funding needs.

While most of the observations made here apply with equal force to all lenders, the emphasis now is placed on the special category of traditional clearing banks.

Lending methods
Clearing banks lend essentially by three basic methods:

- The personal relationship
- Closer planning and control

- The use of financial and other covenants.

In some countries it is the practice for bankers also to pool the lending responsibilities between a syndicate of banks, in which case there is likely to be one lead bank that briefs the others.

The personal relationship basis of lending is all but dying out. Known sometimes disparagingly as the 'Old Boy' basis it results from a position of great trust and confidence between lender and borrower. The business will be well established and apparently secure and healthy, and meetings will take place over lunch without a proliferation of accounts and papers on the table.

The customer will explain his future schemes and explain what problems he is facing, and how he intends to overcome them. The banker will ask relevant questions and sometimes offer advice. Provided he is sufficiently impressed with the business acumen of the manager, and the results published from time to time, the lender will be satisfied with this informal relationship. Any new funding requirement will be discussed as the meeting comes to a close. A shrewd potential borrower may have one or two other options which he may quote to secure the best deal on such occasions.

This informal banker/client relationship is declining, largely because of the less than satisfactory exposure banks have encountered in recent years. It is also the result of the trend that banks are adopting to centralize lending negotiations in regional offices. These are staffed by specialists, and the role of the individual branch banker has been restricted to dealing with day-to-day routine and smaller advances.

Funds advanced on a planning basis are made available on the strict understanding that detailed business plans are submitted and discussed. As the business continues in its trade its proprietors will be expected to attend fairly regular meetings at which any variants from the plan will be explained. The banks will justify this by saying that it is their money at risk (which is true) and that such meetings will give them the opportunity to contribute to solving any problems.

This is not quite so cosy as the first basis of lending which has been described. For one thing one explanation can lead to another two questions. The time can sometimes be better spent in actually attending to the problems within the business than describing them to your backers. The notion that bankers can help you with advice has limited application. For one thing it is not their area of expertise, and in the author's experience they seldom contribute a great deal beyond the obvious and are never willing, in any case, to take on a commercial management responsibility. If you do not believe this, put them to the test and ask them straight out what they themselves would do in any given situation – as though you were asking them to take the decision. They will normally shrink from the task.

This may sound harsh, and it has to be tempered with the particular experience you encounter with your bankers. If they cannot help directly they can often be instrumental in introducing you to those who can. At the worst they always make an excellent sounding board.

The final category of lending is one where you are obliged to enter financial and other general covenants. You may, for example, be obliged to promise that you will not borrow more than a certain amount in total from all sources. You may find yourself liable to repay the advance if you fail to reach a given level of profit. There may be other performance covenants.

Covenants of a more general nature may include a promise not to pledge any assets as security, or to provide regular information in a stipulated form by certain dates, and so on.

In this form of borrowing you are well and truly tied down and at some risk if the industry falters or some other external event influences matters, not to mention your own performance. The banks will argue that this is also for your own good: 'If there is a problem the sooner we all discuss it the better.'

This is all very well but some banks that are very strong on marketing and seeking new business are often the first to pull out and leave you struggling at the first sign of trouble. These will be the banks with all the covenants on their word processors.

It tends to be the banks that have taken longest to give up the old traditional method of lending that are most likely, in the author's experience, to support you in the longer term through difficult patches.

Other considerations

Very high on the list is the regard that lenders have for your integrity. Of similar importance is their need to satisfy themselves that you have full confidence in the project being financed and your own ability to achieve success.

If you are encountering times of trouble they will be far more impressed if you reveal the nature of your difficulties to them – the more so if you have remedies that sound convincing.

If you share a problem in this way and give them the opportunity of making their own observations, you will be much better supported if you consequently take a knock. It is almost as though you and your lenders alike have become parties to the proposed action. If you were wrong so were they!

They will be anxious to see that you are technically qualified, as far as necessary, for the responsibilities you carry in your own capacity. It will add to their confidence in you if you arrive promptly for meetings, smartly dressed and with a reasonably outgoing and cheerful personality. They will not admire you if you talk down to them, are secretive and avoid the line of discussion that they are leading.

If you have developed a full business plan along the lines we have discussed earlier they will be delighted to know that the business is being run along methodical and controlled lines. This may be sufficient in itself to avoid the formal 'planned borrowing' basis we have discussed.

Your performance at meetings is crucial. Prepare what you want to say in advance, do not be verbose and remember not to leave without covering every aspect that you intended. Bankers are never ruffians and they expect you to act like a gentleman.

It is essential that your credibility stands the test. If you do not know the answer to a question, say so. If you promise to explore the point you will be held in better regard than if you take a wild guess or lie, and you will build on the knowledge in anticipation of that question next time.

It is good practice to prepare a written checklist of all the standard questions concerning the business, together with those that you anticipate will arise following publication of the results of each quarter or half year. Add to the list those questions that catch you out. You will find that it will be shorter than you imagine, and you can refer to it to reinforce your memory before the meeting. Its use extends beyond meetings with banks to shareholder meetings, stockbroker lunches and press conferences, if your business is large enough to hold them. You will soon become an expert.

Your credibility will plummet if you turn up with imprudent and crazy schemes and ambitions that defy all logic. Whatever you propose it must be seen to be logical and responsible. If it is quite irrational it will be immediately exposed. Be consistent unless changing circumstances have led you to change your views. If so, say so. Expect to negotiate. Know what the market is offering and what you might expect elsewhere.

The best practice is to wait until the bank gets around to the subject of whether you wish to borrow any more money. The author never refuses invitations to a bank lunch, partly because the food is always good and partly because it presents such opportunities as these. Talk about anything you like, but avoid asking for cash.

As the lunch moves towards the end the manager is likely to ask 'Is there anything else we can do for you? which, translated, means 'Can we lend you any more money?'

These words are music to the ears of a prudent treasurer or finance director. That 'little' question puts the initiative firmly in his court.

If you can wait to be asked you have the initiative in the negotiations which follow. Be coy at first and promise to consider it against any need and other alternatives. Do not show indecent haste and you will land the best deal.

How much do we need?

If you do not know the answer to this you should not attend any meeting in the first place.

If you go away saying that you do not feel there is a current need, and then rush back next week, you will be viewed with great suspicion to say the least. Bankers and other lenders prefer to lend to managers that know their business and their business needs. Otherwise it strikes terror into them.

There are always fluctuating needs. The best way of avoiding embarrassment and covering these is to borrow above your requirements, ie by raising your cash headroom. By this we mean your on-line available facilities and not your theoretical borrowing ceiling, however calculated.

Prepare your full business plan and read it well. It will provide you with the answers. For subsequent events update it by the continuing use of rolling forecasts built into your accounting system.

How do we ask?

If you are not fortunate enough to receive the approach first from the potential lenders you will have to make personal contact. This will be directly and with known sources unless you are introduced by a third party to unknown contacts. Never attempt to discuss the matter by telephone.

The meeting arranged, you will arrive on the due date with your presentation already rehearsed. If the meeting is a more casual one with present contacts you will have prepared your case for verbal presentation and the rest will flow from there.

If the purpose of the advance is to finance a new venture or business, or something out of the ordinary it is essential that your presentation is much more attractive. It will involve you in presenting information that you would prefer not to if you wish to conduct the matter on the easy-going basis first described. But if you are not known to the lender, and the project is at all complicated, you simply will not obtain the requisite funds on the basis of a friendly chat. Your lender will undoubtedly have to refer to others, and it is good discipline for you to prepare a complete dossier on the matter for your own benefit in any case.

Such a dossier will contain:

- A summary of the proposal
- A page or two on any past history
- An explanation of how the opportunity has arisen and what it constitutes
- An explanation of the nature of the business
- Your strategies
- Market analysis information on the size of the market and the applicant's current or future role in it

- Brief details of the management team
- An organization chart if applicable
- Details of any material contracts
- Three years' past accounts if available
- The forward business plan
- A statement of cash requirements
- A list of assumptions behind the plan
- Any available visual display, product catalogues, photographs, slides or press cuttings.

If a number of potential lenders are being addressed a well-presented series of slides can work wonders. Issue the bound material described above afterwards or you risk losing their attention. You may decide to circulate the binder in advance of the meeting.

Let your lenders know that you have prepared for this presentation and give them the opportunity of attending it in the proposed form.

Invite interested parties to attend the place of business so that they can see what is going on at first hand. This will help them to identify with the product and understand matters discussed at a later date. It will also give you an opportunity to show off your strong points. This level of presentation will serve to convince your lenders that you have thought the matter out very carefully and that you have a methodical mind. It is all information that they are likely to request in any event sooner or later. Much time can be saved by appearing with the information in the first place; you do not always get a second chance.

When asking for large sums of money it will not serve your purpose well if you fidget and look embarrassed. Early in the author's career his employers were turned down for what seemed a minor amount of money. The chief executive took the lead in the conversation and failed to offer any specific plans or purpose for its use other than 'we need it to pay our overdue bills etc'.

It is a paradox in the money market that you can most easily obtain finance when you need it least, and the opposite is true with greater emphasis.

At a later meeting it could be demonstrated that matters had begun to improve, and detailed plans were submitted regarding the use to which the money would be put. This was all supported by a business plan, albeit of an immediate short-term nature. This time a request for a much more significant sum was made without blushing, and agreed instantly. Meantime, the chief executive still managed to redden up and, choking, nearly fell off his chair at the amount requested and its immediate approval. It was a moment to treasure.

The best advice is therefore:

- Be well prepared
- Show confidence
- Ask in good time before it becomes too crucial and denied
- Try to ask on an upturn in fortunes
- Request more than you strictly need
- Know the 'nitty gritty' options of any loan as best you can before you negotiate
- State your requirements or expectations with regard to the terms of the loan. If you cannot contemplate a commitment fee or early repayment provision say so *now* before it gathers momentum
- Keep your cash headroom rolling in front of you.

What to expect

You can expect to be closely cross examined on the material which you have presented. If this is contradicted by you now or later you can expect to be quizzed on this. Remember that the basic rudiments of you discussions will be entered in the minutes of any well organized lender, and particularly the banks. Colleagues who put a different slant on what you have said, or tell a different story, are a pain which you can do without.

If you have made a good presentation you can expect to be treated with respect and warmth. You will be informed, usually, that the matter will now be referred, and you can expect the lender to indicate the date when an answer will be forthcoming. This will involve a committee meeting if the sum is at all material – the higher the sum the more senior the committee.

If it is agreed in principle a draft contract will be prepared, at which time it is essential to iron out the many terms which will be included in the small print. A good or bad deal will hang heavily on the small print.

The more you can demonstrate that you are in command of what you want the better are your prospects of success – but do not crow about this at all costs. If you are at deadlock remember those concessions that you can make that will do you no harm.

The author has frequently been asked to agree to a covenant which restricts the granting of specific security to other parties. This is known as a negative security pledge. There is nothing more likely to limit your capacity to borrow than a balance sheet cluttered with notes about security given to various parties. Once each piece of the balance sheet has been pledged you have no more to offer. If, on the other hand, you accept the negative pledge there is no such limitation. Other more important concessions can then be won.

By obtaining this agreement the banks were happy that they had achieved a considerable coup. The reverse is actually the case because you can use this covenant to ward off any other such requests indefinitely from all other parties. The coup in these circumstances is yours, not the bank's, but you can make it win. The absence of security pledges enhance, not diminish, your capacity to borrow.

If the application for an advance or loan is turned down some explanation is normally given. You should reflect on this and decide for yourself whether the rejection made good sense. It may have been to do with the particular circumstances of the bank at the time, in which case you may be told the particular reason also.

Let these matters determine your next step. If you now go forward to another potential lender you will be that much better prepared.

What do bankers look for?

Bankers will first be looking for the kind of information included in our presentation above.

Next they will be looking at other information they may hold on the prospects and position of the industry in the economy at large. If they are prejudiced against a particular industry then your case will be harder to argue, but with luck your sphere of operation may be the flavour of the month.

We have already said that they will be looking for the right personal qualities such as integrity and confidence. They will be interested in the track record of the management team and the accord with with which they all work together. We are now past the days when the words 'divorced or separated' were entered on the record as being fair indication that the borrower will be distracted from the task in hand.

It is true that bankers will try to get a feel for the personality with which they are dealing. They will certainly want to feel that they can conduct a sensible and positive conversation with him, and that they are getting truthful replies to their questions.

They are normally apprehensive if there is not a reasonable representation of accountants or similar professionals on the directing committee, and they will want to see evidence of business maturity, judgement and acumen. Bankers will test the figures provided to see how they conform to the more important health tests we have discussed.

In particular they will be looking at the specialist banking ratios which were mentioned earlier, namely:

- Interest cover
- Leverage
- Break-up value.

They will have their own current view on what standards should be achieved in these areas. If you want to know how you conform they may be quite willing to tell you if you enquire. Broadly speaking, banks will be cautious if interest is not covered by pre-interest profits by a factor of two.

Leverage expectations may go as high as 280 per cent before serious concern is shown provided the operation is trading profitably.

Once gearing passes 67 per cent in the UK they will normally start to worry, although it is not uncommon for it to rise even to 100 per cent in some countries. It is useful therefore to enquire into local practice in the country of operation.

Break-up values go towards propping up under par performance elsewhere. They help in the overall assessment and may be looked at in order to provide additional comfort. The total break-up value will certainly have a profound influence upon the level of security required. We are not so much dealing with ratios and relative performance here as absolute values.

Banks are bound to have regard to your gearing level. Of all the general ratios and health checks discussed this is likely to be the one they centre on most of all because it directly influences the risks being taken and the interest cover.

If your capacity to borrow is limited by a level of gearing which is already high it will influence your chances. If it is not prudent for them then it will not be so for you.

Your own, and the business track record, are bound to be scrutinized. They will attempt to discover from you just what other lines of credit you have available to you from other sources. This will give them a feel for how well borrowed you may be, and also serves as their own market intelligence. This is not the kind of information that you may want to reveal if you are introducing an element of competition between them, or if you want to impress them with the need for the facility when you have others which are for the moment unused. This is your safeguard, but if they are at all cautious about making the advance this information may give them some well-founded excuse, without offending you too deeply. Whether and for how long you can withhold this kind of information depends largely on your relationship and your relative strength.

Just as profitable but cash absorbing companies receive accolades in the financial press, so too can bankers be influenced. However, lessons are being taken from their experiences in industry and having an enlightening effect.

If they decide to make an advance they will then turn to your borrowing limitations to ensure that there is no kind of legal impediment preventing them from proceeding.

This could be in the form of:

- Limitations imposed under the Articles of Association
- Limitations imposed under the terms of any debentures or special share classes
- Covenants given to other lenders restricting the amount which can be borrowed in total at any time.

If you do not have these at your own fingertips at all times you are courting disaster.

Imagine their disbelief if you do not know how much you are entitled to borrow under terms with which you should be completely familiar. They will then turn to the level of security you can offer.

It is not enough for a smaller business to be able to show that it is profitable, and profit *potential* will be viewed with greater concern.

It is usually not enough that the business has assets in it which, upon realization, may cover the advance. There is the risk that some other party may commence the action first, and the possibility that the bank may be competing with others in any liquidation.

Last but not least is the bother and expense of having to go to such lengths to retrieve funds which are fully at risk and yet which earn only a small proportionate return when viewed individually.

This will all lead to the inevitable request for directors' guarantees and other security. The most common of all forms of security in the UK is that of pledging the deeds of your freehold private property. Other regular methods are to attach a charge to investments such as endowments or other funds.

Bankers will always look for a proportion of security cover, not necessarily to give them total protection, but binding in the interest of the borrower.

It will always be the most unpalatable request. It can mean, in the last resort, that you can lose your home if your business venture fails. The bank's view will be that they are not obliged to risk losing their money. If they make it available it is for you to decide how confident you are in pledging it to your business use.

You may be so full of optimism that the draw of the business potential is so strong that you may not give this a second thought. If possible keep the security you pledge to the very minimum. If the lender becomes sufficiently anxious to participate in the opportunity then you may well do very much better than first suggested.

Remember that business failures often occur for reasons beyond your anticipation, influence or control. Your security or home will be required by your family. This may not be as serious as you think. In many parts of Europe the practice is to rent accommodation rather than to own it.

It must be said that obtaining security-free monies can be like getting blood out of a stone. Far better if the security required is inherent in the business. If you are buying one that is undervalued, for example, the answer may well lie in the freeholds and other assets that the business already owns. It is a question of using your tenacity to the fullest degree.

What should the parties expect from each other?

As a minimum the banks expect your full cooperation, integrity, loyalty and best endeavours to make your business a success for the mutual benefit of both parties. They will assume, in other words, that you are driven by the profit motive.

At the other extreme they may wish to tie you down with numerous covenants, unwelcome intervention, and the security of just about everything you own.

It will all depend on the bank and the particular relationship that you both initiate and develop later. Their future trade comes from the reputation and regard in which they are held. They want to be seen as fair in everything they do and they set their own standards even higher than those they expect from their customers.

A pledge, whether verbal or otherwise, once given, is seldom withdrawn. The circumstances would have to be unusual indeed.

For the customer's part he will expect fair dealing, and most of all support for his business when times are bad and it is most in need. He will look for the keenest terms and the usual high standards of day-to-day service of his account. He will not of course welcome shock news such as the sudden withdrawal of his facility, nor will he be too pleased about unexplained charges arriving on his account.

6

The Future Now

The way forward

Now is the time to take stock of all the elements of our business that we have subjected to the closest scrutiny.

Our self-appraisal has helped us to understand our:

- Personal values, motivations and objectives
- Style and means of management
- Management skills and requisites
- Organizational abilities and other qualities.

The look at our general business health has revealed:

- Signs that are there for us to read
- Our risk status
- Performance in all areas of the business
- Adequacy of our controls
- How we have scored against numeric standards.

The analysis of the business driving forces have shown us:

- The dynamics which operate in a changing environment
- Our break-even point and margin of safety
- The business capacities and limitations
- Our total business structure and ways of improvement.

The look at the future has revealed:

- Where inertia is taking us unless we change things
- The value of financial models
- The use of spreadsheets and desk-top computers
- Whether there are problems ahead

- Reasons for success or failure to which we can relate.

Our look at action possibilities has shown us:

- The approaches we might take towards success
- How to recognize lost causes and mistakes
- How to organize our action programmes.

As a result we will have determined the following:

- Our action priorities and how to approach the task
- How to complete a business plan for a healthy concern
- How to read the risks and sensitivity of our position
- The means of motivating our employees.

For the future we are well prepared to:

- Safeguard our position
- Obtain and secure adequate funding levels.

You will not have to confront any particular area of difficulty to take advantage of the principles described herein. Your business may be one of the most profitable and successful but you may still find within these pages some means of raising the return on your investment. If so we will have achieved what we set out to do.

A practical way forward now would be to take the key areas summarized above and return to any section of the book where you are still in doubt. Further research, contemplation and discussion may be necessary before you decide on the application.

It is unlikely that you have stopped at each chapter and carried out the suggested work as you have progressed through it, and less likely that you will have put the book down to complete a full inertia forecast or business plan before reaching the end. Now is the time to review all that we have touched on, and to follow through the desirable action in the recommended sequence.

When you reach the conclusion of your business plan then you will want to secure your funding. It will be better to arrive at your bank with this in hand, but there is nothing that says that you cannot call a meeting to obtain advice or sound out the bank at an interim stage.

Remember the basic steps:

- Review
- Measurement

- Analysis
- Inertia forecast
- Business plan
- Action
- Funding

If you have the following personal attributes:

- Sound commercial judgement and business acumen
- Good negotiating and motivation skills
- A good grasp of the above basic steps

then you have all the essential ingredients for formidable success!

It will help if you have a business with sound inherent strengths, or if you have a good business idea. But with the above attributes you have probably selected a winner in the first place.

You can now make your own luck!

The upward cycle threat

We draw to the end with a warning relating to the upward cycle threat.

If the action we have taken has been forced upon us because of poor profits and cash flow we may be in a particularly vulnerable position as we come out of the troubles.

During the action period we will have concentrated to a large extent on creating extra liquidity. It is likely that cash will have poured in to a far greater extent than normal as we have shed labour, de-stocked, stemmed losses by eliminating products with negative margins and so on.

It is possible that this cash flow left us feeling a little more optimistic than was prudent. The truth is that the cash flow benefits may be short term, and as we now revert to 'normal' trade two things may happen:

- We may not have done enough and a negative cash flow may return.
- As we re-expand our stocks will be replenished and cash extracted from various areas may be sucked back in again.

Quite the most dangerous scene is one where a business has encountered difficulties, experienced a cash rich period during the action process and then re-expanded quickly on its freshly charted course.

If you were to draw this on a graph it would take on the appearance of a horseshoe. The most critical moment of danger is just as you are going into the upturn. It is the more critical because your former condition will have brought some concern from your staff, customers and bankers alike.

If you are now seen to be in difficulty again at so early a stage in your recovery then you may not this time have the requisite support, even though your future appears rosy through your own eyes. Such a business is in a far worse position than one which has run out of steam on a straight line expansion course. You might argue that it could be better to start again than run into this cruel trap.

It can be referred to as the upward cycle threat. It is important to learn the lesson and to take strenuous avoiding action. This will normally include as a minimum:

- Exaggerated cash saving action initially
- Care to ensure that the costs of the action are fully planned (not forgetting redundancy pay, closure costs etc)
- Patience to slow down the rate of re-expansion until you are quite clear of the danger zone.

For those businesses that have experienced problems, the risk of falling down at this late stage are too disappointing to contemplate. Avoid them at all costs.

Index